FORD RS ESCORTS

Other Titles in the Crowood AutoClassics Series

AC Cobra	Brian Laban
Alfa Romeo Spider	John Tipler
Aston Martin: DB4, DB5 and DB6	Jonathan Wood
Aston Martin and Lagonda V-Engined Cars	David G Styles
BMW: Classic Cars of the 1960s and 70s	Lawrence Meredith
BMW 3 Series	James Taylor
BMW 5 Series	James Taylor
BMW M-Series	Alan Henry
Carbodies	Bill Munro
Citroën 2CV	Matt White
Citroën DS	Jon Pressnell
Datsun Z Series	David G Styles
Ferrari Dino	Anthony Curtis
Jaguar E-Type	Jonathan Wood
Jaguar Mk1 and 2	James Taylor
Jaguar XJ Series	Graham Robson
Jaguar XJ-S	Graham Robson
Jaguar XK Series	Jeremy Boyce
Lamborghini Countach	Peter Dron
Land-Rover	John Tipler
Lotus and Caterham Seven: Racers for the Road	John Tipler
Lotus Elan	Mike Taylor
Lotus Esprit	Jeremy Walton
Mercedes SL Series	Brian Laban
MGA	David G Styles
MGB	Brian Laban
MG T-Series	Graham Robson
Mini	James Ruppert
Morris Minor	Ray Newell
Porsche 356	David G Styles
Porsche 911	David Vivian
Porsche 924/928/944/968	David Vivian
Range Rover	James Taylor and Nick Dimbleby
Rolls-Royce Silver Cloud	Graham Robson
Rolls-Royce Silver Shadow	Graham Robson
Rover P4	James Taylor
Rover P5 & P5B	James Taylor
Rover SD1	Karen Pender
Sunbeam Alpine and Tiger	Graham Robson
Triumph TRs	Graham Robson
Triumph 2000 and 2.5PI	Graham Robson
Triumph Spitfire & GT6	James Taylor
TVR	John Tipler
VW Beetle	Robert Davies
VW Transporter	Laurence Meredith

Ford RS Escorts
The Complete Story

Graham Robson

First published in 2000 by
The Crowood Press Ltd
Ramsbury, Marlborough
Wiltshire SN8 2HR

**British Library Cataloguing-in-
Publication Data**
A catalogue record for this book is available
from the British Library.

ISBN 1 86126 374 0

Acknowledgements

I've got a problem here. Escorts have been a part
of my life for so many years that hundreds of people – yes, really – have helped me to understand,
analyse, and enjoy the cars.

I could start, therefore, by saluting Walter
Hayes and Stuart Turner – two of the earliest
influences – carry on by mentioning Keith Duckworth, Brian Hart, Rod Mansfield, Bob Howe
and Mike Moreton, remember far-flung owners
such as Derek Wickett of Australia, and end by
listing every Ford club enthusiast who has ever
shown me a car.

But I would probably end up ignoring countless others – from Ford, to the club scene and not
forgetting the enthusiasts' world – who have all
been so very helpful.

But I must make a special case. Towards the
end of this saga, I could not have found dozens of
new-to-me pictures without the help of Jim
Fowler and Fran Chamberlain of Ford's Photo-
graphic Department. Only they know what a
nuisance I was, and only they could have guided
me so helpfully to the correct files.

My thanks, therefore, go out to Ford enthusiasts, all round the world. I hope the result is
worthwhile.

Typeface used: New Century Schoolbook.

Typeset and designed by
D & N Publishing
Membury Business Park
Lambourn Woodlands
Hungerford, Berkshire.

Printed and bound in Great Britain by the
Bath Press.

Contents

Escort RS Evolution   6
Preface   8

1   Inspiration – 'Total Performance' and the Lotus-
    Cortina   9
2   Escort Twin-Cam and RS1600 – Mk I Marvel   21
3   Mexico and RS2000 – Blood Brothers from AVO   45
4   Second-Generation RS – RS1800, RS2000 and
    RS Mexico   61
5   The 'Works' Escorts – Motorsport Miracles   83
6   Hopes Dashed – Escort RS1700T   107
7   Front-Drive Fireworks – RS1600i and Escort RS Turbo   119
8   Front-Wheel-Drive Racers – in Motorsport   141
9   ACE – the Escort RS Cosworth   155
10   Escort RS Cosworth and RS2000 in Rallying –
    not Forgetting the Escort WRC   169
11   Escort RS2000 and 4×4 – 16 Valves for the 1990s   187

Index   205

Escort RS Evolution

January 1968	Introduction of new Escort range, including Escort Twin-Cam
January 1970	Introduction of new Escort RS1600. Twin-Cam continued in production
November 1970	Escort RS1600 assembly (but not Twin-Cam) transferred to new AVO factory at South Ockendon, Essex
November 1970	Introduction of Escort Mexico
Spring 1971	End of Twin-Cam assembly at Halewood
Autumn 1972	From this point, RS1600 engines were equipped with aluminium cylinder blocks
July 1973	Introduction of Escort RS2000. Initial assembly at AVO and also at Saarlouis, Germany
October 1973	UK market sales of Escort RS2000s began
December 1974/ January 1975	Closure of AVO plant announced. Assembly of all Mark 1-shaped Escorts ended
January 1975	Preview of Escort RS1800. Initial batch production began at Halewood later in the year
March 1975	Preview of Escort RS2000 Mark II
January 1976	Official introduction of Escort RS2000 Mark II, along with introduction of Escort RS Mexico Mark 2. Assembly at Saarlouis, Germany. From this point, Escort RS1800 'production' was by converting RS Mexico Mark IIs at South Ockendon
Autumn 1977	End of batch production of Escort RS1800
September 1978	End of RS Mexico Mark II assembly. RS2000 revised into 'Base' and 'Custom' models
July 1980	End of all rear-wheel-drive Escort production. Last assembly of RS2000 Mark II
October 1980	Design work began at Boreham on the Escort RS1700T, a projected 200-off Group B car
September 1981	Preview of Escort RS1600i, to be built at Saarlouis, Germany. Sales of left-hand-drive cars began shortly after

Escort RS Evolution

October 1982	Announcement of right-hand-drive Escort RS1600i, for sale in UK market
March 1983	RS1700T project cancelled, at pre-production stage
Summer 1983	End of RS1600i assembly
October 1984	Announcement of Escort RS Turbo, with sales beginning at the end of the year
November 1985	End of original-style Escort RS Turbo assembly
July 1986	Announcement of revised Escort RS Turbo, with styling facelift and engineering changes
Summer 1990	End of production of Escort RS Turbo
September 1990	Preview of new-generation Escort RS2000, and of Escort RS Cosworth
November 1991	Escort RS2000 sales began. All production centred at Saarlouis
May 1992	Sales of Escort RS Cosworth began. All assembly centred at the Karmann factory in Germany
September 1992	'Smiley-face' style changes announced for entire front-wheel-drive Escort family, including RS2000. No changes to the Escort RS Cosworth
March 1994	Introduction of RS2000 4×4, with four-wheel-drive, additional to front-wheel-drive model. Sales of left-hand-drive cars began at once, but UK sales were delayed until July 1994
May 1994	Announcement of revisions to Escort RS Cosworth, including use of small-turbo engine.
January 1995	Final facelift ('Mark VI') for the front-wheel-drive Escort, including new nose, new fascia, stiffer bodyshell. Applied to RS2000/RS2000 4×4, but not to the Escort RS Cosworth
January 1996	Escort RS Cosworth model discontinued
November 1996	Announcement of Escort World Rally Car, strictly motorsport-only derivative of Escort RS Cosworth, to be used only in rallying
December 1996	Final Escort RS models – RS2000 and RS2000 4×4 – discontinued
November 1998	Final appearance by a 'works' Escort, the Escort World Rally Car, in the RAC Rally of Great Britain

Preface

I've always wanted to write a book about Ford's famous RS-badged Escorts – I've owned them, driven them, and loved them – but for years I had to keep on holding back. Until the late 1990s, this was an on-going story, yet I wanted to tell it all. It had, in other words, to be a 'Complete Story'.

Happily, for every Ford enthusiast, there always seemed to be a good reason why that wasn't true. Every time I got enthused, gathering together my facts, my figures, and my pictures – and starting to talk to Crowood about this book – Ford moved the horizon yet again, by announcing yet another new model.

The bad news finally came in 1996, when the last two cars – the rally-winning Escort RS Cosworth, and the front-wheel-drive RS2000 – came to the end of their careers. Ford told us that falling sales and ever-tightening legislation had killed them off, but I knew better.

This, I concluded, was no more and no less than a death due to Old Age, for the entire RS concept had enjoyed a wonderful, near 30-year, run. It meant that I could finally link all the cars together – starting with the Escort Twin-Cam of 1968 and ending with the final models of 1996, linking their histories with the inspiration behind them – and relive the years when they did so much to reinvent Ford's entire image.

This, make no mistake, is also a very personal story. RS-badged Fords have been a part of my daily life for more than twenty years and I've owned several types (the most exciting being the Escort RS Cosworths I enjoyed in the 1990s), always using them as day-to-day transport. Even though the RS badge was abandoned in 1996, at the time of writing there is still a mid-1990s RS2000 in my garage.

I wish I could also claim that I had driven every different type but, like most of you out there, I never got close enough to an RS1700T to do that. On the other hand, I drove several 'works' rally cars when they were in their prime, and I reckon that's a bonus!

This is a wonderful story, which has never been told before, and I hope I have brought the romance to life. The bad news may be that Ford has abandoned the RS side of its business, but the good news, surely, is that thousands of the cars – even the ultra-rare ones – have survived into the new century, and will provide enjoyment for decades to come.

So, as at least one of the one-make magazines always says: CheeRS!

Graham Robson, 2000

1 Inspiration – 'Total Performance' and the Lotus-Cortina

This is a long and fascinating story. For every Ford enthusiast, the 'RS' label was in their life from 1970 to 1996. Choose almost any year and there was an Escort involved somewhere.

Over the years, RS-badged Escorts set new performance standards, captivated the hearts of enthusiasts all over the world – and sometimes redefined the market they were contesting. No other manufacturer ever achieved what the 'RS' – Rallye Sport – label did for Ford. Not always simple, but enthralling. Not always successful, but invigorating. Always offered with passion – this is a story as much about people as it is about machines.

Although the first RS-badged Escort appeared in 1970, its ancestors were conceived nearly ten years earlier. The founding father, no question, was Walter Hayes, his muse was Colin Chapman of Lotus, and the engine that seemed to make everything possible was the original Lotus twin-cam.

A long way from the RS1600, and the Cosworth-designed BDA engine? Indeed, yes, but without them I doubt if anything else would have followed.

HAYES + CHAPMAN = DYNAMITE

This story really began in 1962, soon after Walter Hayes had arrived at Ford, to establish a new-style Public Affairs department. Walter once told me:

At the time I was Associate Editor of the *Daily Mail*. I told my wife that what I would really like to do was to take a three-month sabbatical – and then decide what I might do.

Sir Patrick Hennessy, Ford's chairman, then asked me to see him ... he wanted somebody on the board who really knew about politics, and the way the world was changing.

Sir Patrick needed to replace his Public Relations chief, ex-World War II SOE hero Col. Buckmaster but: 'I said "Public Relations? Well, I don't really know a lot about that"...' – which, I reckon, must be one of the most unlikely disclaimers of all time!

We agreed a little cautiously that I would go to Dagenham, and that if we liked each other after a year, then I would join the board. Hennessy said to me: 'Well, since it isn't going to be Public Relations, we will call you Director of Public Affairs.'

Having moved into Dagenham in December 1961, and found his bearings, Hayes then started to get more pro-active. As one of his colleagues, Harry Calton commented:

Walter arrived, but we weren't told very much. This small man arrived, and sat in his corner office, with his typewriter ... he then started to hire people. He'd been given a clean sheet of paper. As he said afterwards, he had no budget and no direction, so therefore he followed his own instincts ...

The Lotus-Ford twin-cam engine was the power unit which sparked off the high-performance Escort family. Brand new in 1962, it was at its peak when the Escort Twin-Cam was conceived.

And what instincts! Using a combination of journalistic flair and (as he cheerfully admitted to me, many years later) almost total ignorance of the 'Ford system', he began to transform Ford's public image.

Almost by accident, it seems, he discovered that he was also responsible for overseeing Ford's motorsport activities, which were being carried out in a distinctly parochial manner. With cars based out at the Lincoln Cars building in Brentford (on the A4, on its way out to London Heathrow airport), sharing space and personnel with the press-car fleet, and with Publications Manager 'Edgy' Fabris spending part of his time looking after the programme. Hayes insists:

It wasn't a programme with any real sense in it. Rallies themselves were gentlemen's activities – and half of Ford's 'works' team drivers seemed to be Ford dealers anyway!

But people like 'Cuth' Harrison and David Haynes were dead keen. I let them go on for a bit, with Zephyrs, but we then started doing competitions with the Cortina.

Which is why Hayes immediately got together with Colin Chapman of Lotus, who had his own ambitions:

I'd found Chapman when I was still running the *Sunday Dispatch*. I wanted a different slant on cars. He wrote for me, but he was difficult in many ways: you could never get the copy out of him ...

Hayes, though, was always impressed by Chapman, by his appealing (if demanding) character, and by his dynamic way of getting things done. Chapman, it seems, had already been in touch with Ford, because of a new twin-cam engine he was having designed.

Starting in 1961, Chapman had hired Harry Mundy (technical editor of *The Autocar* – and one-time chief designer of the famous Coventry-Climax F1 and F2 twin-cam racing engines) – to design a new twin-cam cylinder head to fit on to the bottom end of Ford's new Anglia 105E/Classic 109E engine.

By 1962 this project had moved swiftly forward, by using the still secret longer-stroke 1.5ltr version of the same engine, which not only had a bomb-proof five-main-bearing bottom end, but was destined for use in the forthcoming Cortina. Chapman's plan was to have this engine ready for October 1962, for use in a new sports car – the Lotus Elan.

Things then moved swiftly. No sooner had Hayes joined Ford than Chapman started nagging away for a closer involvement, and it was only a matter of months (mid-1962)

before the two of them conceived an extremely important new model – the Lotus-Cortina.

There are several different versions concerning who did which, when, and first (Terry Beckett, the 'Mr Cortina' product planner who later became Ford's Chairman, reckons that it was as much Ford's idea as Chapman's), but the most persuasive is that Hayes, determined to revitalize Ford's motorsport image, consulted Chapman first.

Together, it seems, they worked out a brilliant scheme for a new Ford 'homologation special', which could be raced, and which could have the beating of the Jaguars which currently had a stranglehold on Saloon Car racing.

For Hayes and Chapman, the secret was all in what was already being developed. Lotus (with the help of Keith Duckworth at Cosworth) was already finalizing the twin-cam engine, based on a Ford pushrod engine that just happened to be destined for use in the soon-to-be-announced Cortina, while Ford was about to reveal the ultra-light

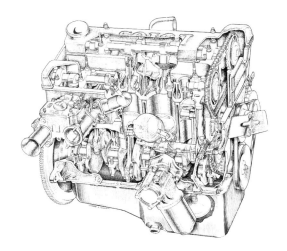

Obsolete by twenty-first century standards, the Lotus-Ford twin-cam engine was very advanced when designed in 1961. When race-tuned, a 1.6ltr version could produce up to 180bhp. It fitted neatly into an Escort body shell, too!

Walter Hayes

Between 1961 and 1989, when he finally retired, Walter Hayes was one of the most dynamic and enthusiastic supporters of all high-performance Ford programmes. Yet, by his own admission, he was really a newspaperman and not a motor industry executive, and latterly a publicist rather than a motorsport administrator.

Already famous as an editor in the world of British newspapers, he joined Ford to revolutionize their public face. Originally in charge of Ford UK's Public Affairs department, and soon the influence behind every motorsport programme, he modernized Ford's thinking in every way. It was Hayes who found the money to build the Boreham motorsport centre, who urged Ford to finance Cosworth's DFV F1 engine, approved the launch of the Escort Twin-Cam, lobbied hard for the opening of the Advanced Vehicle Operation, hired Stuart Turner as his new Director of Motorsport – and much more.

By the 1980s he had become Vice Chairman, Ford-of-Europe, brought back Stuart Turner from the Public Affairs operation, kept the Sierra RS Cosworth in being when others had gone wobbly on it, and did more than anyone to make sure the Escort RS Cosworth went into production.

When he reached his sixty-fifth birthday he retired, for that was Ford's global ruling, but he was not yet ready to forget about cars. One of his later tasks was to become Aston Martin's chairman, to get the new DB7 project approved, and generally to revive yet another struggling organization.

Guru? Of course. Inspiration? Certainly. Influential 'top brass'? Naturally. But also a deep thinker, a visionary, a motoring enthusiast – and a very important man. Without him, in my opinion, the history of Escort RS cars might have been extremely short – maybe non-existent.

Without Walter Hayes of Ford (left) or Colin Chapman of Lotus, there might never have been an Escort RS story to tell. That is an 8-valve Lotus-Ford twin-cam engine.

Cortina, of which a high-output Cortina GT was already planned.

The Hayes-Chapman 'master plan' was for Lotus to re-engineer the Cortina GT model, not only by slotting in its own Lotus-Ford twin-cam engine, but by using many light alloy body panels (which would be supplied by Ford's own pressings plant at Dagenham), plus a new Lotus-developed rear suspension system.

Not only that – and this is where Chapman's ambition came together with Ford's vision – but the cars, at least 1,000 of them, to ensure Group 2 sporting homologation, would be assembled at the Lotus factory in Cheshunt, to the north of London.

Rushed through against a near-impossible timetable, the Lotus-Cortina (or the Cortina-developed-by-Lotus, as Ford insisted on describing it for years after every enthusiast had stopped listening) was previewed in January 1963, then put on sale as rapidly as possible, with homologation pushed through so that the 'works' teams could start beating the Jaguars!

MK 1 DEVELOPMENT – A COMPLETE REDESIGN

The first Lotus-Cortina was very different from the 'base' Cortina – though later production cars would get progressively less special as the months and years passed. Starting from a Cortina two-door body shell with many aluminium skin panels (the assembly being delivered to Lotus as a complete, white-painted, shell), Lotus added its 105bhp twin-cam engine, backed it by a Cortina GT gearbox containing the close-ratio Elan ratios, and fitted transmission assemblies with light alloy clutch bell housing and rear axle nose piece castings.

The rear suspension was completely revised. Not only were leaf springs discarded, replaced by coil-over-damper units, but there was substantial tubular stiffening inside the shell to stiffen up the shell mountings, the axle being located by a combination of twin trailing radius arms and an 'A-Frame' which was tied to the axle nose piece. Other special touches were the spare wheel bolted to the floor instead of tucked to one side, and the battery which also lived in that area.

Add to this the lower and stiffened suspension, the 5.5in width steel wheel rims, the new fascia panel display and the aluminium doors, bonnet and boot lid panels, the standard colour scheme of Ford white with Lotus green flashes on the sides and across the tail, and the Lotus badges (even though this was still officially a Ford, covered by the Ford warranty!), and here a was a distinctive and very promising sports saloon.

Although the Lotus-Cortina was launched in January 1963, deliveries, in numbers, did not begin until mid-1963. This was for two reasons – one being that development of the original design had not yet been finalized, the more important being that the new Cortina GT (on which much of the 'chassis' was based) was not itself due for introduction until April!

Nevertheless, as soon as it was homologated (in September 1963 – which was a long, long way in advance of the necessary 1,000 cars being produced) the Lotus-Cortina was a competitive race car. No less a personality than F1 Champion Jim Clark used 150bhp

Team Lotus 'works' cars to win the British Saloon Car Championship in 1964 – and Ford's long-running race track success story was under way.

On the track, however, and especially on the road, there were many teething problems, connected with the rear axle, and most specifically with that special rear suspension. As Roger Bell of *Motor* later wrote:

> Characteristically, this car wriggled and writhed like a drunken sidewinder on anything but smooth surfaces, fidgety steering movements being the order if its wanderings were to be kept in check.
>
> We reckoned the A-frame glued the back end down so well, the front always lost grip first, resulting in safe and consistent understeer ...

One of Walter Hayes's first actions was to inspire the birth of the Lotus-Cortina, which was the original 'Fast Ford'. This is Bengt Soderstrom and Gunnar Palm on the Monte Carlo rally of 1966. The Escort Twin-Cam was still two years into the future.

Until the 1960s, Ford did not manufacture a high-performance engine. The Lotus-Ford Twin-Cam, conceived by Harry Mundy and originally used in the Lotus-Cortina, changed all that. Bulky twin-choke Weber carburettors meant that this was a very wide engine.

Even on tarmac roads, the combined shock/spring mountings gave the shell a hard time (bump and shock loads were fed into the original shock absorber mounting turrets, which had not originally been intended to withstand them), this meaning that kinks appeared in that area. Until, that is, Lotus beefed up the stiffening arrangements. More serious was the tendency of the continuous pushing and pulling of elements in the rear suspension A-frame to cause the axle casing bolts to loosen off and let out all the oil. Shortly, and inevitably, the crown wheel and pinion set would fail.

On early cars this problem was so serious that it caused a scandal. *Autocar*'s sports editor, Peter Garnier, collected a very early-build car in May 1963, ran it as a staff car for 29,000 miles, and eventually lost all patience with it.

Even though, because of his position, he had the 'inside track' to Lotus, his car still suffered no fewer than six rear-axle failures,

not to mention the rear suspension collapsing three times – all these problems being directly related to the 'Lotus' rather than the 'Ford' parts of the car.

In the first two years, therefore, many changes were forced through, some not very well-known. Special Equipment cars were provided with 115bhp engines, and were little publicized at the time. From July 1964 a two-piece propeller shaft took over from the one-piece, most light-alloy panels and castings were abandoned (though they were still kept in reserve, for fitment to racing versions), and a wider set of gearbox ratios was fitted. From October 1964, the latest 'Aeroflow' type of body shell was standardized, with full-width grille and through-flow ventilation.

By early 1960s standards these were supremely fast, exciting and wickedly-attractive new Fords, and there always seemed to be a stream of customers ready to forgive all their failings. As Harry Calton told me, Ford was quite relaxed about them:

The Lotus-Cortina started racing and winning in September 1963, and it marched over everything else in sight, and that was enough. We could keep on saying: 'But it's winning, it's winning ...' and the people who bought them were ready to live with all the problems.

Reliability usually wasn't an issue as far as they were concerned ... when it was running, and it was on song, it was super, and that seemed to be enough. The dealers lived with this.

Next, in June 1965, came the most important change of all, which translated this machine from a troublesome Lotus to a super-fast Ford Cortina. The A-frame suspension was abandoned in favour of the Cortina GT's leaf spring plus radius arm set-up: this was surprisingly effective. Finally, from October 1965, yet another set of gearbox ratios was used, those being the 'Corsair 2000E' ratios. This, incidentally, was the point at which left-hand-drive versions were officially built.

This change, incidentally, was resisted by those who thought that nothing which Ford had designed could possibly work as well as anything by 'genius' Chapman. Ford then arranged a series of back-to-back tests at the Snetterton race track, with Vic Elford and 'Gentleman' Jack Sears driving representative cars. Sears, in particular, was considerably quicker when driving the leaf-spring version, and that really clinched the reason for change.

Because the Cortina was about to be restyled, and because Ford was disenchanted by Lotus's poor quality standards at Cheshunt (after one early visit, one Ford quality-control inspector was supposed to have said: 'I don't think they have a single torque wrench in the place ...'), Lotus was informed that they would not be building the next-generation cars. Colin Chapman,

for whom the Lotus-Cortina contract had been extremely profitable, was furious.

Accordingly, the last of 2,894 Mk Is (about 1,800 of these were 'leaf spring' cars, incidentally) were produced at Cheshunt in the autumn of 1966, after which there was a six-month marketing gap with no Lotus-Cortinas on the market.

This was caused by the fact that the new-style Cortina Mk II had gone into production, and because a new Lotus-Cortina derivative was not ready. Ford eventually announced the Lotus-Cortina Mk II in March 1967, a very different type of sports saloon, which it proposed to build at Dagenham, among other Cortinas, so that it could be seen to comply with Ford's ever-rising build quality standards.

Looking back, I am sure that this was as big an influence on the birth of the first 'hot' Escort – the Twin-Cam – as any other. Whereas I don't think that anyone at Ford ever considered trying to produce a Lotus-engined version of the Anglia 105E which ran alongside the first-generation Cortinas, the fact that Ford could produce a relatively reliable – civilized, even – Lotus-Cortina Mk II made all the difference.

By the time the Dagenham-assembled Lotus-Cortina Mk II went on to the market, all the bugs had been shaken out of the Lotus twin-cam engine, its transmission and the lowered suspension which was fitted into that car.

LOTUS-CORTINA MK II – THE RS ESCORT'S ANCESTOR

Having driven lots of them, I've never understood why the Mk II has been 'talked down' in later years, for it was an excellent, all-round, fast sports saloon. In almost every way than in outright straight-line speed, it was a better car than the Mk I –

better built and better equipped – with a more roomy cabin.

There wasn't any doubt, though, that some of the quirky made-by-Lotus character had gone missing. What was really a twin-cam engined Cortina GT Mk II, somehow, lacked the charisma of an individually-designed Mk I, even if you knew the axle wasn't going to let you down, and that you would usually get to the end of your journeys, short or long!

A Lotus-Cortina GT-based Mk II shared the same rounded, two-door style of the new-style Cortina GT, the same basic mechanical layout, fascia style, and the same leaf-spring/radius-arm layout, and could be ordered in a whole range of monochrome colours (then, if the customer demanded this, a contrasting 'speed stripe' could be added in the Ford dealer's paint shop).

This time the twin-cam engine was supplied in Special Equipment guise: once quoted by Lotus at 115bhp, Ford always quoted a more realistic 109bhp (net). As with the last Mk Is, there was a 2000E type of gearbox, but this time the axle ratio had been raised a little – 3.77:1 instead of 3.90:1, just 3.5 per cent higher, but worthwhile.

All cars had lowered/stiffened suspension and 5.5in wide-rim steel wheels and,

The Lotus-Cortina Mk II of 1967 was a great car, but it was a bit too large and too heavy to be a motorsport winner. Even so, almost everything under its skin – engine, transmission, axle and front suspension – would be crammed into an Escort body shell for 1968!

for the very first time, they were equipped with 165-13in radial ply tyres. The spare wheel was mounted upright at the side of the boot (as with other Cortina Mk IIs), but the battery still had its own tray on the boot floor, and was connected to the engine bay by a long armoured cable running under the floor of the shell.

Not as special as the Mark I? Maybe – but the customers didn't seem to see it that way. In little more than three years, far more Mk IIs were made than Mk Is had ever been – Ford claims 4,032 examples were made, all of them on the tracks at Dagenham, where they jostled for space with Cortina GTs and other less exciting types – and these were in production until July 1970.

Even so, the glamour faded, and the steam really went out of the programme, after the Escort Twin-Cam went on sale in the spring of 1968, for many enthusiasts turned to that car instead. Only 194 cars were built in the final calendar year.

In those three years, important Mk II changes were limited to the fitment of a new fascia/instrument panel layout from October 1968 (like all other Cortinas at the same time), and there was a new type of 'single-rail' remote control gearshift control from that point. This, incidentally, was the point at which the car was officially re-named 'Cortina Twin-Cam' (with Escort Twin-Cam-style badges to suit), though once again this was a name used more by Ford than by their customers. To them, a Lotus-Cortina was a Lotus-Cortina, and that was the end of the discussion.

There was no question about the effectiveness of this model, as *Motor* magazine testers suggested about the Mk II in 1967: 'Anyone in the market for a £1,000 saloon who doesn't buy a Lotus-Cortina must be mad ...'.

Boreham

Once an orchard near Chelmsford, Ford's Boreham site became an airfield in the 1940s, a motor racing circuit in 1950, a proving ground for Ford trucks from the mid-1950s, and the home of Ford Motorsport from 1963.

Boreham opened as a military bomber airfield in March 1944. After the war, the airfield was speedily decommissioned, then from 1950 it was used as a motor racing circuit by the West Essex Car Club.

Ford then took over the site in the mid-1950s, for use as a heavy truck test and development centre, and installed many special facilities.

When Walter Hayes arrived at Ford in 1962, he decided to revitalize Motorsport. On a budget of just £32,000, a new centre was built at Boreham, where Motorsport operations began in mid-1963.

Then, as later, the 'works' team could use the airfield for test and proving purposes. For more than twenty years, Boreham was shared between Motorsport and Truck Development (later the Ford New Holland development facility), but all truck activity ended in the late 1980s. Motorsport then moved into the former Truck Development offices.

Motorsport originally operated 'works' Cortina GTs and Lotus-Cortinas. The original Escort Twin-Cam was designed there in 1967, and the first of the 'works' Escort rally cars followed in 1968. Hundreds of victories, and Championship successes, ensued. A number of 'works' race cars – Capris and Escort RS1600s – were also based in the same workshops.

Design and development of several limited-production Ford cars, notably the RS200, the Sierra RS500 Cosworth and the Escort RS Cosworth, was also carried out at Boreham along with (in more recent years) the Escort WRC and the latest Puma Racing types.

Henry Taylor

Henry Taylor was the farmer who took up motor racing, became Ford-UK's competitions manager, and finally ran a thriving boatyard in the south of France.

Taylor started racing in 1954, advanced to F2 by 1958, drove for Britain's bobsleigh team at St Moritz, and later even dabbled briefly in non-Championship F1 events.

Then, in 1961, he began to drive in Ford's 'works' rallying team, and when Alan Platt moved out he then became Ford Competitions Manager from 1965 to 1969.

It was under Taylor's control that the Lotus-Cortina became a winning rally car, that heroes like Roger Clark, Bengt Soderstrom and Ove Andersson joined the team – and when the Escort Twin-Cam was invented. Guided by Walter Hayes, Taylor also signed up Ralph Broad and Alan Mann to run successful saloon car racing teams.

When AVO was set up in 1969, Taylor moved to take charge of various high-performance engine programmes, but in the early 1970s he finally left Ford and moved to the Mediterranean, where he bought and expanded a profitable boat yard, and was still running it at the start of the 2000s.

prototypes of a humble little saloon car being driven past his office window. According to legend – and I am sure it is true, for so many other people have confirmed the tale – one day Bill stopped, button-holed his team manager Henry Taylor, and said: 'Blimey, one of those things would go like hell with a Twin-Cam engine in it!'

It took over a year for Meade's fantasy to turn into limited-production reality – even at 'can-do' Ford in the 1960s, miracles took time to complete – but that single sentence was always the essence of the new car. The Escort Twin-Cam was basically no more than a lightly re-engineered Escort two-door shell with Lotus Twin-Cam gear in it.

Authentic badges like this were often stolen from Twin-Cams in the early days – often re-appearing on mundane Escort 1100s, which didn't fool anyone.

PLANNING, TESTING, CRASHING ...

One Sunday morning in January 1967 – the twenty-fifth actually, which is where the project code really did come from – Henry Taylor got together with the existing Lotus-Cortina Product Planner, Bob Howe, who later told me:

> Before then, there was no such car in the product plan. Walter Hayes, who I had never even met, sent for me, told me he wanted to do such a car, asked me if I was interested, and sent me to see Henry. There was no time to tackle the job in normal working hours, so Henry asked if I would go out to his big house in Wickham Bishops.

We spent a whole day writing out the requirements, and the objectives. Nothing like this had been done at Ford before – the Lotus-Cortina had been planned inside 'mainstream' Product Planning. No-one else in Product Planning, I reckon, would have wanted to take on this job: it was really a Bob Howe baby. But I don't think anyone could have done it if the Lotus-Cortina hadn't already been out there, winning.

Public Affairs chief Walter Hayes knew what was going on, but did not interfere. When the time was ripe, he would start the lobbying process at which he was supreme.

It was the first of many requests which would flow from Boreham to the company's HQ at Warley in the next two decades, and all

Interesting! XTW 368F, which later became a rallycross car, was shown to the motoring press in Morocco in January 1968, complete with its non-standard Rostyle wheels. Note the Zodiac 'chase car' lurking in the background.

This was Cosworth's 16-valve twin-overhead-cam FVA Formula Two engine of 1966, a direct ancestor, but very different in detail from the RS1600's BDA unit. No BDA ever had gear-driven camshafts.

had the same theme – the team needed a new world-class competition car, but also needed to see it put on sale. In short, they needed a new 'homologation special', which meant that 1,000 road cars would have to be built.

Although no-one had even built a car to prove the theory, it was a simple idea. The Lotus-Cortina was a race and rally winner, but the forthcoming Escort was lighter, smaller and stronger. So, why not graft the Lotus-Cortina's running gear into an Escort body shell, to produce a potentially better car?

Somehow, Taylor and Howe managed to 'borrow' a prototype Escort body-chassis unit, in plastic, from Ford's technical centre, and in one frantically busy weekend at Boreham, Meade and his mechanics proved that it was feasible. Meade told me:

We stopped all normal work on a Friday afternoon in March 1967 when the 'car' arrived in a truck. We shut the workshop doors, started there and then, and spent all weekend, mocking up a new car.

Sounds simple, doesn't it? Remember, though, that the plastic shell, undamaged, had to be returned after the weekend, and that the Lotus-Cortina running gear was all more bulky than the Escort was intended to accept.

Somehow, with a lot of sweat, swearing, and a few bruised knuckles, the Twin-Cam engine and gearbox, the Lotus-Cortina struts and rear axle, all found a home, but the engine had to be mounted at an angle to gain clearance between carburettors and inner wheelarch, the battery had to be relocated in the boot, while the 165-13in tyres only just fitted inside arches designed around 145-12in rubber! There were no drawings, no photographs, but just a few measurements, notes and sketches – and high hopes.

A few months later a running prototype was built – this actually being a press-tool try-out shell which Bob Howe procured. This car was soon written off when a body-shell weld broke on an early test run – not Boreham's fault, thank goodness. In the meantime

Hayes finally gained approval to have the car put into production, on the basis that Boreham must complete the development on its own.

In only six months, between rallying outings with the Mk II Lotus-Cortinas, the 'works' mechanics built, tested and proved a handful of prototypes, and in January 1968 the very first publicity car – XTW 368F – made its debut at the Escort launch in Morocco. The reason for the rush was simple – Henry Taylor needed to bounce the car through the FIA's homologation procedures with great despatch, for he wanted to see the new car rallying, and racing, as soon as possible in 1968.

Except for the engine-bay problems, and the need for some 'big hammer' treatment around the gearbox tunnel to make way for the bulky Cortina-style gearbox, the Lotus-Cortina mechanical kit fitted surprisingly well; except for finding the battery on the floor of the boot, with the fat spare wheel sitting alongside it, the customer would never see where the space problems had occurred.

So far, so good – but how on earth were the 1,000 cars to be built?

TWIN-CAM – BUILDING THE FIRST CARS

The new bread-and-butter Escort was to be manufactured at Halewood, a suburb of Liverpool (the plant which would eventually be its home for the next 32 years), though there was no planned place for a limited-production 'special' to take shape on the same lines.

No matter: Hayes, Taylor and Howe started nagging – and kept on nagging. Reluctantly (most reluctantly, as Bob Howe and Walter Hayes both recalled in later years), Halewood management agreed to assemble the cars, using strengthened 'Type 49' body shells, keeping them on normal assembly lines up to a point, then whisking them away to a special area known as a 'crib', where specially-trained fitters fitted engines, gearboxes and axles – and road tested every completed car.

For simplicity's sake, *every* production Twin-Cam was to be painted white, with black trim, and every car would have right-hand drive. Bob Howe told me:

Bob Howe

If ever he retired (which, at 70 years of age in 2000, he had still not done), Bob Howe was likely to have an unparalleled track record at Ford.

First as an assembly-line worker at Dagenham in 1951, and later as junior in Terry Beckett's Product Planning Department, by the mid-1960s he was the Product Planner on the Lotus-Cortina Mk II.

Bob was drafted in to make planning sense out of the Escort Twin-Cam project, was the first Ford employee to drive a car powered by the BDA engine, the planner sent out to find a factory for the AVO operation, and the first employee of that new organization.

In the early 1980s, he was attracted back to Motorsport to look after legislation programmes on the mid-engined RS200. After which he personally sold every one of the cars, and clocked up more miles in them than anyone else!

Ready, once again, to retire in 1989, he repeated the legislation trick for the Escort RS Cosworth. Later in the 1990s, he worked on various Ford schemes, including an ambitious Ford recycling project.

One day, he admitted, he might think about retiring, but with a fiftieth anniversary approaching in 2001, not just yet.

This cutaway show engine reveals the very heart of Ford's new BDA engine – four-valves per cylinder, a narrow angle between those valves, and a twin-cam layout. In the 1990s, as in the 1960s, most 16-valve engines stuck to this basic architecture.

Someone later calculated that for every Twin-Cam built down the line at Halewood, we lost one-and-a-half standard Escorts! After the Twin-Cam, they said: 'Never again. No more. Ever.'

There was no way that Halewood could begin assembly – even in penny numbers – until the spring of 1968. Yet Henry Taylor wanted to get the car homologated for motorsport before the season began (by May 1968, could he convince the FIA that 1,000 cars had been built, even when fewer than 100 actually existed? He thought he could – and, in the end, he did ...) and agreed to have the first twenty-five 'production cars' assembled at Boreham; journalist Barry Gill, newly recruited to Ford from Fleet Street, got the job of allocating the cars. Almost all of these went to favoured motorsport teams like Alan Mann Racing, and one or two overseas customers; one or two became road test cars, while Boreham kept the balance for its own use. Priced at £1,123 for sale in the UK – that was exactly

the same price as the Mk II Lotus-Cortina, by the way – the Twin-Cam was sure to sell well, just as soon as cars could be delivered.

The first motorsport appearance was in rallycross, at Croft, in January 1968.

For the Escort RS1600, the BDA's bottom end was almost pure 'Kent', while the aluminium cylinder head, the belt-driven camshafts and the twin side-draught Weber carburettors were all pure Cosworth.

Group 3 homologation (500 cars completed – or so Ford claimed) was achieved only six weeks after launch, on 1 March 1968, and Ove Andersson drove a car in Italy's San Remo rally later that month. Group 2 homologation (1,000 cars built, which was another fiction …) was finally achieved on 1 May 1968.

Lotus-Ford twin-cam engine

Colin Chapman of Lotus hired *The Autocar*'s Harry Mundy in 1961, to design a new twin-overhead camshaft engine based on the new Ford 105E/109E pushrod cylinder block. Mundy had been chief designer at the world-famous Coventry Climax concern in the 1950s.

Mundy's concept design was detailed by Richard Ansdale, and the very first engine ran in November 1961, the original five-bearing 1,498cc unit following in May 1962.

Keith Duckworth of Cosworth finalized the cylinder head, porting and camshaft design, and when series production began at the end of 1962, the engine was a 1,558cc/105bhp unit.

Manufacture was originally by J A Prestwich of North London, but after Lotus relocated to Hethel, Norfolk, in 1967, manufacture was taken 'in house'. This was the engine that went on to power the original 'hot' Escort – the Twin-Cam.

Before then, of course, this engine had been fitted to thousands of Elans, Elan Plus 2s, and of course Lotus-Cortinas. Yet by the time the Escort Twin-Cam was launched in 1968, its breathing limitations were already known, which explains why it was soon replaced by the first of the Cosworth-designed 16-valve BDA power units.

Approximately 34,000 such Lotus twin-cam engines were manufactured, the last being produced at Hethel in 1975.

Feast your eyes on the anatomy of the new 16-valve BDA engine, and compare it with the FVA shown on page 25. Simpler in almost every way, and with belt-driven instead of gear-driven camshafts, the BDA would have a long, successful, and altogether distinguished career.

TWIN-CAM ON THE MARKET

Twin-Cam assembly built up very slowly indeed, but Taylor cheerfully told white lies over homologation. He knew, and Walter Hayes knew, that more than 1,000 would be built eventually – and that there was a market for them – and in any case motorsport success was more important to them than the minutiae of regulations.

At the end of the car's career – spring 1971 – the requisite numbers had probably been achieved, but at the time Ford never provided detailed figures for us to analyse.

Many years later, I was given an authentic list of actual Escort Twin-Cams and RS1600s that were produced at Halewood from 1968–70 – this information being an extract of reliably authentic Ford/Halewood month-by-month production documents. Here is the relevant section:

Month	Production Total	Production Domestic	Production Export
1968			
March	1	1	–
April	25	25	–
May	36	36	–
June	33	33	–
July	30	30	–
August	26	26	–
September	43	43	–
October	13	13	–
November	67	67	–
December	28	28	–
302 cars, in total, built at Halewood in 1968			
1969			
January	65	65	–
February	22	22	–
March	5	5	–
April	52	52	–
May	60	60	–
June	44	44	–
July	50	50	–
August	14	14	–
September	19	19	–
October	52	52	–
November	48	46	2
December	48	45	3
479 cars, in total, built in 1969			
1970			
January	34	28	6
February	15	15	–
March	8	8	–
April	3	3	–
May	9	9	–
June	17	17	–
July	9	9	–
August	5	5	–
September	2	2	–
October	Separate Twin-Cam figures no longer detailed		
November	Separate Twin-Cam figures no longer detailed		
December	Separate Twin-Cam figures no longer detailed		
102 cars, in total, from January–September 1970			

Although Twin-Cam assembly continued slowly and fitfully until the spring of 1971, no further details were ever issued from Halewood, or from anywhere else at Ford. Accordingly, the total number of Twin-Cams to have been built at Halewood was 883, and the grand total must have been about 1,000. Belated, but finally honest!

No-one who drove a Twin-Cam was ever disappointed, which is as good a proof of its 'father of Escort RS cars' status that I can give. Except that these white two-door saloons had wide-rim 13in wheels with fat tyres, front quarter bumpers, and discreet little 'Twin-Cam' badges, they were almost impossible to pick from their smaller-engined brethren. Over the years a lot of rubbish was talked about 'flared wheelarches' to clear those fatter tyres, but even after all these years I still don't think this change was very significant.

Once on sale, Ford spent little time and effort on the improvement of the Twin-Cam. Indeed, except that original cars were sold with rectangular headlamps, while those

F1 World Champion Graham Hill, and AVO manager Ray Horrocks drive the first AVO-built RS1600 off the assembly lines on 2 November 1970. Hundreds of RS1600s had already been assembled at Halewood.

Escort Twin-Cam (1968–1971)

Layout
Unit construction steel body/chassis structure. Two-door, front engine/rear drive, sold as four-seater sports saloon.

Engine
Type   Lotus-Ford Twin-Cam
Block material   Cast iron
Head material   Cast aluminium
Cylinders   4 in-line
Cooling   Water
Bore and stroke   82.55 × 72.8mm
Capacity   1,558cc
Main bearings   5
Valves   2 per cylinder, directly operated by twin overhead camshafts and inverted bucket-type tappets, with camshafts driven by chain from the crankshaft
Compression ratio   9.5:1
Carburettors   2 horizontal dual-choke Weber Type 40DCOE
Max power   106bhp @ 6,000rpm
Max torque   107lb ft at 4,500rpm

Transmission
Four-speed manual gearbox, all-synchromesh
Clutch   Single plate, diaphragm spring

Overall gearbox ratios
Top   3.77
3rd   5.28
2nd   7.58
1st   11.20
Reverse   12.52
Final drive   3.77:1 (Hypoid Bevel)
(17.8mph (28.6 km/h) /1,000rpm in top gear)

Suspension and steering
Front   Independent, by coil springs, MacPherson struts, track control arms, and anti-roll bar
Rear   Live (beam) axle, with half-elliptic leaf springs, radius arms and telescopic dampers
Steering   Rack-and-pinion
Tyres   165-13in radial-ply
Wheels   Steel disc, bolt-on fixing
Rim width   5.5in

Brakes
Type   Disc brakes at front, drums at rear, hydraulically operated.
Size   9.62in front discs, 9.0 × 1.75in rear drums

Dimensions (in/mm)	
Track	
Front	52.7/1,310
Rear	52.0/1,320
Wheelbase	94.5/2,400
Overall length	156.6/3,980
Overall width	61.8/1,570
Overall height	53.0/1,346
Unladen weight	1,730lb/785kg

UK retail price	
At launch in 1968	£1,162.78 (+ £8.31 for front seat belts, which were 'compulsory' extras)

built after July 1969 had 7in (177.8mm) circular headlamps (which gave better night vision, but which according to Ford's bosses meant that the car was no longer as up-market!), there were virtually no other development changes. If anyone complained about the lack of colour choice – and there must have been a few – they were politely told that there was no alternative: some ultra-trendy buyers, I hear, actually had a respray after taking delivery. If they had waited to 1970–71, when the last cars were being put together at Halewood, a choice of colour was finally available.

TWIN-CAM ON THE ROAD

When the Twin-Cam was a current model, I often enjoyed driving one. To me, keen, impressionable, and captivated by the car's character, every time was like the first time, and my adrenalin raced. There was that extrovert and matchless rush off the line, wheelspin and all, to reach exciting cruising speeds. There was the immensely eager way the steering turned the chassis in to any corner (Boreham's engineers had seen to that, for later work on RS Escorts

showed how easily the chassis could be persuaded to understeer). There was also the unmistakeable engine noise, the gobble of carburettor throats, and the high-pedigree thrash of valve gear.

A Twin-Cam was at its best on country roads, or being rushed up and over the mountains – any road, in fact, where the 106bhp engine's torque, and the agile handling, could dominate the drive. Put a Twin-Cam out on a motorway, on the other hand, and it was really out of its element, because this was a low-geared car that didn't always like to run straight in cross-winds.

Nevertheless, with its 110mph (177km/h)-plus top speed, and its sub-10 second 0–60mph (0–100km/h) acceleration potential, it was an outstanding little machine, one which inspired the birth and development of later Escorts.

Even at the end of 1969, when the Twin-Cam was still in its prime and selling steadily, its successor the Escort RS1600 had already been designed, and there was never any intention of transferring Twin-Cam assembly from Halewood to South Ockendon.

No matter. When the Twin-Cam finally faded away in April 1971, its character lived on in the RS1600 and other AVO models. Today, quite simply, it is remembered as the First, and the most Famous.

WHO INVENTED THE RS1600?

The RS1600 which succeeded the Twin-Cam was another magnificent 'homologation special', a taut little two-door saloon with which I fell in love on the first occasion I took it along a twisty lane in Essex. It was a car that meant so much to Ford and the company's sporting dominance of the 1970s.

Yet according to today's performance standards, an Escort RS1600 isn't a very exciting car. After all, it 'only' does 111mph (179km/h) – whereas a 1990s-style Escort RS Cosworth could approach 140mph (225km/h). The Escort RS1600 thrummed up to 100mph (160km/h) in about 32 seconds, whereas an Escort RS Cosworth made it in about 17 seconds. What does it prove? It proves damn all – except that I shouldn't have dug out the figures in the

first place. In 1970, when the RS1600 was announced, I was already writing about cars and, believe me, I can still remember what a stir it caused.

The very first time I drove an RS1600, I was working for a rival concern. This was no secret, and Ford's staff was happy to let me borrow one of their demonstrator cars: I was actually running the product proving department at Chrysler-UK. The Hillman Avenger GT had just been announced, the very first prototype 16-valve Avenger-BRM (do you remember that?) had just been built, and Chrysler's directors wanted to see how it matched up to Ford's new baby.

Without telling Ford too much, they said, could I borrow an RS1600 to be tried, and compared? 'No problem,' the engineer said. 'If you lend us an Avenger GT, you can have an RS1600. Will a week be long enough?' He then blew away all my discretion by adding: 'Does that mean you've got the BRM engine into a car, then?' Then, as now, the industry grapevine was healthy …

I drove down from Coventry to Essex in an Avenger GT – and came back in the

Spare wheel bolted to the floor, battery in the spare wheel well – these were identification points of all early-generation Escort RS1600 and Mexico types.

Escort RS1600 (1970–1974)

Layout
Unit construction steel body/chassis structure. Two-door, front engine/rear drive, sold as four-seater sports saloon.

Engine

Type	Ford-Cosworth BDA
Block material	Cast iron (Cast aluminium from late 1972)
Head material	Cast aluminium
Cylinders	4 in-line
Cooling	Water
Bore and stroke	80.97 × 77.62mm (sometimes quoted as 80.97 × 77.72mm, for sporting homologation reasons)
Capacity	1,599cc (sometimes quoted as 1,601cc, for sporting homologation reasons)
Main bearings	5
Valves	4 per cylinder, directly operated by twin overhead camshafts and inverted bucket-type tappets, with camshafts driven by cogged belt from the crankshaft
Compression ratio	10.0:1
Carburettors	2 horizontal dual-choke Weber Type 40DCOE (2 Dellorto DHLAE from April 1972)
Max power	120bhp @ 6,500rpm
Max torque	112lb ft at 4,000rpm

Transmission
Four-speed manual gearbox, all-synchromesh

Clutch	Single plate, diaphragm spring

Overall gearbox ratios

Top	3.77
3rd	5.28
2nd	7.58
1st	11.20
Reverse	12.52
Final drive	3.77:1 (Hypoid Bevel)

(17.8mph (28.6km/h)/1,000rpm in top gear)

Suspension and steering

Front	Independent, by coil springs, MacPherson struts, track control arms, and anti-roll bar
Rear	Live (beam) axle, with half-elliptic leaf springs, radius arms and telescopic dampers
Steering	Rack-and-pinion
Tyres	165-13in radial-ply
Wheels	Steel disc, bolt-on fixing
Rim width	5.5in

Escort RS1600 (1970 – 1974) *continued*

Brakes
Type   Disc brakes at front, drums at rear, hydraulically operated.
Size   9.62in front discs, 9.0 × 1.75in rear drums

Dimensions (in/mm)
Track
    Front   52.7/1,310
    Rear   52.0/1,320
Wheelbase   94.5/2,400
Overall length 156.6/3,980
Overall width   61.8/1,570
Overall height 53.0/1,346
Unladen weight 1,920lb/870kg

UK retail price
At launch in 1970   £1,446.56 (+ £8.49 for front seat belts, which were 'compulsory' extras)

Starting in the autumn of 1972, RS1600s were fitted with the aluminium cylinder block that Brian Hart had developed. For motorsport it could be enlarged to a full 2ltr engine size. It also saved a claimed 40lb/18kg in weight. Dellorto carburettors replaced Webers at about this time too, but never on competition units.

Yet it was short-lived. Born in a rush of enthusiasm, the AVO factory at Aveley (sometimes called South Ockendon) closed down after only four years. Not profitable, Ford said. But if the enthusiasts had been right in 1970, were the accountants right in 1974?

Bob Howe, who was Ford's original AVO employee, thinks that everyone was right:

We certainly sold all the cars we could build until the energy crisis hit us hard. After that, sales fell, the bean counters told us we were losing money, and closure was inevitable.

Later, as Bob told me:

J25 – the Twin-Cam – was causing considerable disruption at Halewood, and I was told to find a new place, outside the company as we knew it, to build such cars.

Egged on by Walter Hayes, Bob's strategy paper, dated June 1969, proposed a new facility to 'produce performance versions of production cars'. It was always intended to be a profitable venture, or it would speedily have been rejected.

After looking round most of Essex, it seems, a Ford-owned building at Aveley,

The AVO project

What eventually became the Advanced Vehicle Operation (AVO) had been developing in Walter Hayes' fertile brain since 1965. Although cars were only built at South Ockendon from 1970 to the end of 1974, this business-within-a-business is now legendary in the hearts of all Escort RS enthusiasts.

Hayes eventually gained approval for AVO at board level, to set up a new self-contained business in which specialized cars, many of them for use in motorsport, would be built – and that these would be supplied to a new breed of Ford dealerships, known as the RS (or Rallye Sport) chain. AVO was also to spread its tentacles to Ford-Germany, where cars like the Capri RS2600 were to be produced. On Hayes' behalf, Bob Howe viewed no fewer than fifty locations in Essex before eventually recommending an in-house facility, where spare space had recently appeared.

Originally a corner of a vast complex set up by Ford at Aveley/South Ockendon, for engineering and other purposes, it had become redundant as these departments moved to the new technical centre at Dunton. Conversion work began in the winter of 1969–70, and the first car – an RS1600 – was officially driven off the lines on 2 November 1970.

At its peak, AVO employed more than 250 people and – officially at least – the 110,000sq ft (10,219sq m) plant (which cost £329,000) could produce twenty-three cars a day, or around 5,000 cars a year. In fact it was rarely at full stretch, and was never very profitable. One reason for the building of thousands of Escort 1300Es at AVO in 1973 and 1974 was to help spread the financial overheads.

When early enthusiasm was at its height, AVO's team considered making cars as various as the GT70, a 3ltr V6-engined Cortina, four-wheel-drive Capris and Granadas, and even batch assembly of a turbo-Ford-engined DeTomaso Pantera.

After the Energy Crisis struck in the autumn of 1973, and when the mainstream factories found themselves on short time, AVO was always in danger. The last cars were built there at the beginning of 1975, and with the tiny exception of completing a few RS1800s at South Ockendon, almost all the Mk II RS types were produced in Saarlouis.

By the 1980s no trace of AVO remained at South Ockendon.

Ray Horrocks

At the time a merchandising manager at Ford, Ray Horrocks set up and managed Ford's Advanced Vehicle Operation (AVO). It was Ray who made a practical business out of a bright idea from 1969 to 1972.

No sooner had he launched the new Capri in 1969 than Deputy Chairman Len Crossland called him up, made him the AVO offer ('which I couldn't refuse'), and left him to it. To flesh out the business, he drew in experts like Henry Taylor, Bob Howe, Dick Boxall and Mike Bennett as his senior staffers.

Although the sales organization was launched in January 1970, the AVO production lines did not roll until November of the same year. Ray then managed the expanding business – first the Mexico, then the launch of the Capri RS2600 in Germany, a start to the work on the RS2000, a dabble with the GT70, thoughts of building 3ltr V6 Cortinas, a start on turbocharged Granadas and Capris, 4×4 Capris, and other exciting might-have-beens – until 1972.

Headhunted away from Ford by Eaton of North America (to run its British materials handling business) he then lost touch with Ford. He eventually came to run the Austin-Rover section of British Leyland in the early 1980s, and finally moved on to head Chloride plc.

which had just been vacated by another department, was recommended. Taking it over didn't involve significant building costs – in the end the total investment in tools, assembly lines and facilities was little more than £600,000.

AVO had several objectives – to design, develop and build: '… a range of low volume, unique derivatives, for sale by Ford Rallye Sport dealers throughout Europe … to project an image of Ford as a technical innovator… to support the Ford competition effort in Europe by providing vehicle derivatives in appropriate volume …'

For eight to ten months Howe, reporting to Alex Trotman, and keeping Walter Hayes closely informed, was the *only* Ford staffer working on the scheme, and once approval

was achieved, Ray Horrocks became the new department's manager.

Dick Boxall then moved down from Halewood to control the building of the AVO plant (including its famous merry-go-round assembly line, in which body shells were supported on adjustable slings) and to control production. Those slings, incidentally, could have carried any current, or planned Ford model.

At about this time, too, Stuart Turner arrived at Boreham as Competitions Manager, releasing Henry Taylor to look after the development of high-performance engines. Rod Mansfield, later to set up Special Vehicle Engineering in the 1980s, arrived as the fifth employee, to work for Howe on design and development.

Compared with the RS1600, the RS2000 had a much softer, more 'road car', handling package. Much of the development was done by race-driver Gerry Birrell, though the driver of this early demonstrator was journalist Roger Bell.

There was no question of creating a new engine, nor could the 'Kent' engine be made larger or more powerful to fill the bill, so it was time for some 'parts bin engineering'. Fortunately there was another new Ford power unit – the 2ltr single overhead-cam Pinto design – and although it had never been intended for use in Escorts, every effort was made to slot this engine into place. At the same time, it was decided to make the new car, which had already been dubbed 'RS2000' (though 'Puma' was an early possibility), somehow more 'Executive' than 'Rallye Sport' in its general demeanour.

It was a car, in other words, that a young businessman might use for his work, rather than an enthusiast for his pure enjoyment: it was a car more suited to long-distance, high-speed touring than any of the previous Twin-Cam, RS1600 or Mexico breeds. It was, above all, meant to be a car almost as fast as the RS1600, but one which would need only a fraction of vital maintenance.

RS2000 IN DETAIL

In some ways, the RS2000 was very different from either of its AVO-built relatives. By the time the design had settled down, both the engine and the gearbox were not only newcomers to Escorts, but doing a very different job.

AVO's first major problem was to persuade the rather bulky overhead-cam Pinto engine to fit into the engine bay of the Type 49 bodyshell, where at first it seemed to be too long and too deep.

Rod Dyble's engineers found that this could only be achieved by discarding the usual engine-driven cooling fan (a thermostatically-controlled Kenlowe fan was chosen, and fitted in its place), and by designing a new cast aluminium sump pan to fit neatly around the existing Escort cross-member.

In addition, the engine was mounted exactly 'north-south', instead of slightly askew as in previous fast Escorts, this being a 'first' for the developing 'hot' Escort family of cars, and a feature which would follow on in the second-generation cars of 1975–76.

Ford claimed that the change of fan saw the peak power rise from 98bhp (as used in Capris and Cortinas) to 100bhp in the RS2000. I'm not sure that anyone ever

In 1973, RS2000 fascia / instrument panels looked like this, complete with the latest flat-spoke RS-style steering wheel.

Driving comfort, RS2000-style, in 1973, with reclining-type Recaro seats, made the 'office' a very pleasant place to work on long journeys. Thirty years later, Recaro still make the best seats in the business!

measured such a figure – but at least it was a persuasive argument, and looked good when printed in the brochures …

Behind the engine there was a new (to the Escort) type of gearbox, the Type E design from Ford-Germany, which was totally different from that used in RS1600s and Mexicos. Normally to be found behind the Pinto in other Fords, it had different ratios too, with bottom gear being much lower than on the other type. Because it had evolved with the Cortina Mk III (of 1970) and all its successors in mind, this Type E box was important to Ford's future. Further development (and different ratios) would make this box ideal for use in the Mk II Escort RS models of the late 1970s.

The rear axle was the same 'British' or 'Timken' assembly as used on other AVO models, but with a higher – 3.54:1 – final drive ratio.

Compared with the Mexico/RS1600 types, the balance of the ride and handling package was completely revised, especially with a view to reducing the oversteer characteristics, and to soften the ride.

Gerry Birrell, not only a well-respected young racing driver but an accomplished development engineer, was hired to do this job. His first reaction to RS2000 settings was not encouraging. Early one morning, having driven a car at Boreham for the first time, he is reputed to have coasted serenely back to his colleagues, opened the window, smiled innocently, and enquired: 'Is it too early in the morning to be rude?' He then was …

With Birrell's guidance, a series of detail changes were made to the chassis, including different spring and damper settings (the RS2000 had firmer front, and softer rear springs than the other cars). Surprisingly, the rear brakes were made smaller than on the Mexico/RS1600 – 8 × 1.5in (38mm) drums instead of the more familiar 9 × 1.75in (44mm). There was also a new style of

Escort RS2000 (1973–1974)

Layout

Unit construction steel body/chassis structure. Two-door, front engine/rear drive, sold as four-seater sports saloon.

Engine

Type	Ford 'Pinto'
Block material	Cast iron
Head material	Cast iron
Cylinders	4 in-line
Cooling	Water
Bore and stroke	90.8×76.95mm
Capacity	1,993cc
Main bearings	5
Valves	2 per cylinder, directly operated by single overhead camshaft and inverted bucket-type tappets, via steel fingers, with the camshaft driven by cogged belt from the crankshaft
Compression ratio	9.2:1
Carburettors	One downdraught dual-choke Weber Type 32/36 DGAV
Max power	100bhp @ 5,750rpm
Max torque	108lb ft at 3,500rpm

Transmission

Four-speed manual gearbox, all-synchromesh

Clutch	Single plate, diaphragm spring

Overall gearbox ratios

Top	3.54
3rd	4.85
2nd	6.97
1st	12.92
Reverse	12.96
Final drive	3.54:1 (Hypoid Bevel)

(18.7mph (30.1km/h)/1,000rpm in top gear)

Suspension and steering

Front	Independent, by coil springs, MacPherson struts, track control arms, and anti-roll bar
Rear	Live (beam) axle, with half-elliptic leafsprings, radius arms and telescopic dampers
Steering	Rack-and-pinion
Tyres	165-13in radial-ply
Wheels	Steel disc, bolt-on fixing: optional cast alloys
Rim width	5.5in

Brakes

Type	Disc brakes at front, drums at rear, hydraulically operated
Size	9.62in front discs, 8.0×1.5in rear drums

Escort RS2000 (1973–1974) *continued*

Dimensions (in/mm)

Track

Front	52.7/1,310
Rear	52.0/1,320
Wheelbase	94.5/2,400
Overall length	156.6/3,980
Overall width	61.8/1,570
Overall height	53.0/1,346
Unladen weight	1,975lb/898kg

UK retail price

At launch in July 1973: £1,441.82; in October 1973 when UK deliveries began: £1,586.00

Although you never saw this type of Pinto engine in a standard RS2000, Ford got it homologated in Group 1 for use in motorsport from mid-1974. With more than 140bhp, this was a very potent Pinto combination.

four-spoke cast alloy wheel, something which AVO styling had badly needed since it was set up as a separate operation.

Visually, therefore, it was quite easy to 'pick' an RS2000 from its stable mates, even though all the usual AVO features such as quarter bumpers and circular headlamps were retained. Externally, not only were 'RS2000' badges fitted – one on each front wing, one on the boot lid – but the cars were invariably fitted up with startling, but somehow pleasing, colour-contrasting stripes along the flanks and on the bonnets and boot lids. There was also the usual range of body colours. (Need I say that if one nagged hard enough, and loudly enough, it was possible to have a new RS2000 delivered without stripes? AVO was always anxious to achieve another sale ...)

At one time, incidentally, when the talented American Joe Oros was leading the styling team behind this car, studio models were given the name of 'Puma'. Although that idea was abandoned in 1973, the same name would re-appear many years later on the smart little Fiesta-based coupe of the late 1990s.

Inside the car, the ambience was subtly changed – it was a little more 'executive' than 'sporting' – though the standard type of AVO six-instrument binnacle, and the 1973-style RS flat three-spoke steering wheel were both retained. All cars had nicely-shaped reclining front seats, while many had an optional centre console, complete with a clock and provision for a radio installation.

RS2000 ON THE MARKET

The new car was unveiled on 4 July 1973, with the stern proviso from Ford's publicists that all initial production would be of left-hand-drive cars, for sale in Europe. What was not stated at the time was that a large number of such RS2000s were actually assembled at the Ford Saarlouis factory in Germany, close to the French border, at the same time as production was building up in South Ockendon: this was the only time that Mk I RS Escorts were ever built in that plant.

Right-hand-drive versions were released to British customers on 11 October 1973 – just in time to coincide with the outbreak of the Arab-Israeli 'Yom Kippur' war, and the Energy Crisis which erupted from it. This conflict depressed new car sales, and also brought a threat of petrol rationing.

This could not have happened at a more unfortunate time. Even so, at that moment the RS2000 got off to a good start, and was priced at £1,586 in the UK, at a time when the Mexico cost £1,348 (prices had gone up considerably since 1970, for inflation in Britain was on the increase) and the RS1600 £1,864, so the RS2000 did indeed fit neatly into the gap between those two types.

Almost immediately British sales began, there was one important chassis change (which was never emphasized by Ford at the time). This came in November 1973 when all Escorts, including the FAVO types, were given a new type of monocoque platform, with more nearly vertical, rather than steeply angled, rear dampers and turret mountings: I have already noted this in describing the career of the Mexico. Apart from that, a late-model RS2000 Mk I of 1974–75 was much the same as the original version of summer 1973.

Although the original-shape RS2000 would only be in production for about eighteen months, it was by far the car built in most numbers at the AVO plant in that time, so much so that there was a backlog of unsold cars at the end of the year; some were not actually sold and registered until well into 1975.

Figures released many years later show that a total of 5,334 RS2000 Mk Is were produced, 3,759 being sold to British customers. There's no doubt that this short-lived car did exactly what was expected of it,

Yet another RS2000 takes shape on the assembly line at AVO, with the Halewood-made body shell about to be dropped on to the 2ltr Pinto engine.

for Ford's marketing experts were delighted to hear of the type of customers it attracted. RS dealers, too, took to it well, for it was a much more 'service-friendly' car than the RS1600, and much more up-market than the Mexico.

As I make clear in Chapter Five, the RS2000 (especially when running with the homologated twin-carburettor engine) was also a very useful competition car in the right hands and the appropriate events, as Roger Clark (1974) and Tony Pond (1975) proved by winning the Tour of Britain in Group 1 cars.

Those who knew, or who were prepared to find out, discovered that the RS2000 was a

The AVO factory at South Ockendon, in late 1970, just as Mexico production was starting to build up. Using these slings, a wide variety of other models could have been assembled at AVO.

Fascinating! Frua of Italy suggested that this neat little coupé should be built by Ford at AVO, using the Mexico/RS1600/RS2000 platform. It would have cost a lot more money, so would you have bought one? In the end, only the one prototype was ever built.

pleasantly fast car, too, as these road-test comparisons show:

Model	Top speed (mph)	0–60mph (sec)	Standing ¼-mile (sec)
Mexico	99	10.7	18.0
RS2000	108	9.0	17.1
RS1600	113	8.9	16.7

As independent assessments proved, on the open road the RS2000 was almost as rapid as the RS1600 (in fact the 16-valve car was only 2.2 seconds ahead of the RS2000 in sprinting to 100mph/160km/h from rest), yet this was done by using a totally fuss-free, mass-production engine which was widely understood by every Ford dealer's mechanics.

The AVO planners seemed to get it exactly right with their well-matched trio of cars: the Mexico suiting the clubman who wanted more spirit than a mainstream Escort, the RS2000 providing high but reliable day-to-day performance, and the RS1600 providing great potential for motorsport of any type.

My friends at *Autocar* magazine clearly enjoyed their road-test car very much, for their summary mentioned: 'Super flexible performance, good economy and absolutely no temperament.' Their round-up also stated that:

> We make no secret of the fact that we find these high-performance Escorts tremendous fun cars, and for the man who does not want the ultimate in competition machinery, the RS2000 makes a superb road car. On acceleration, top speed and cornering power it can hold its own with much more exotic models and in this respect it is really good value.

That was a considered opinion in 1973, and decades later it still applies to well-preserved examples of the type. After all, do you really need a more common beaky-nose Mark I to make your point?

For all these Escorts, though, the end – when it came – was shocking, unexpected and (to those who could not read a balance sheet) seemingly unfair. After the energy crisis had done its worst, Ford found itself with sharply reduced sales, and the main 'Escort' factories in Britain and Germany were running well short of capacity.

The response, finance-led, but recognized by many of those involved at the coalface, was that AVO now looked to be an indulgence. Manager Stuart Turner was directed to close the place down:

> I got the instruction to shed all but 35 of the AVO workforce [at peak, more than 250 people had been involved]. That was the worst time of my business life. Calling people in to my office and discussing redundancy with them was shattering ...

The news, that AVO would close down as soon as the supply of original-shape body shells dried up, broke in December 1974, and the last cars of all were built in January 1975. This, though, was not the end of the story for the Escort RS, for in recent months ace-planner Mike Moreton had been working out where, and how, the already-designed Mk II models could be made. That is a story on its own, to be related in the next chapter.

The GT70 might have been assembled at AVO. It was conceived in 1970 and following a development period lasting until 1972 it was abandoned after a handful of prototypes were built.

Ford Escort Performance

This is a summary of the figures achieved by Britain's most authoritative magazine, *Autocar*, of Mk I cars supplied for test by Ford over the years:

Model	Escort Twin-Cam 1,558cc 106bhp	Escort RS1600 1,601cc 120bhp	Escort RS2000 1,993cc 100bhp	Escort Mexico 1,599cc 86bhp
Max speed (mph)	113	113	108	99
Accn (sec):				
0–60mph	9.9	8.9	9.0	10.7
0–80mph	16.8	16.1	17.2	20.2
0–100mph	33.6	32.3	34.5	–
Standing ¼-mile (sec)	17.2	16.7	17.1	18.0
Consumption (mpg)				
Overall	21.5	21.5	26.6	27.5
Typical	23	23	28	30
Kerb weight (lb/kg)	1,872/849	1,920/871	1,977/897	1,964/891
Year tested:	1968	1970	1973	1970

4 Second-Generation RS – RS1800, RS2000 and RS Mexico

Mike Moreton summarizes the way in which Mk II RS models were developed. Originally, the project was only to make beaky-nosed RS2000 models, but new-style RS Mexico and 16-valve cars soon chimed in:

Then, in 1974, came the big change, the company had to save a lot of money, so the AVO manufacturing plant was closed down, the workforce was laid off, and we were shrunk to about thirty-five people. All that was left was Stuart Turner, a few of us, and a few engineers: I only had one assistant.

Our remit was simply to introduce the Mk II RS2000, and a Mexico version, which was a much simpler car, especially for Ford-of-Britain RS dealers (it didn't make any sense at all for Germany, France or anywhere else) – and a new RS1800, which Boreham needed for homologation purposes.

Part of the Mk II RS2000 development programme involved the new front-end appearance, which was inspired by Jack Telnack, who had his own agenda for the way he wanted Ford-of-Britain styling to evolve. When Ford-of-Britain wanted an RS Mexico, a much cheaper version, one way to save money was to leave off the special nose, which in our language was good 'product differentiation'.

It was my idea to have RS1800s made by re-engining RS Mexicos at Aveley. It was the simplest way to build a very small number of cars – new engine and gearbox, and

Expecting it to become a best-seller in the late 1970s, Ford gave the Escort RS2000 Mk II a unique nose style, complete with four headlamps. This was an early studio shot of the chosen shape.

new badges, that was about all. All three cars had the same basic running gear – layout, transmission, suspension and brakes.

Even in 1975, we originally planned to build right-hand-drive RS2000s at Halewood, and left-hand-drive cars at Saarlouis, and we started preparing to build the cars in that way. After a while it became blindingly obvious that it really only made sense to build all the cars at Saarlouis.

With the Mk II RS models launched, this left the rump of AVO with nothing else to do, so Stuart Turner moved off to run the Public Affairs department, and Mike slipped back into mainstream Product Planning:

I took what was left of AVO with me, virtually nothing, then wrote a Strategy Paper on 'Specialist Vehicles in Ford-of-Europe', pointing out that specialist cars could certainly be built at Saarlouis, but they needed to be backed by a specialist engineering

The licence plate on this car emphasizes that all RS2000 Mk IIs were assembled at Saarlouis in Germany. The unique nose – four headlamps and a plastic cowl – were blended successfully into the standard shape. This car also has the X-pack body kit fitted – which includes flared front arches, and a unique Zakspeed-style front spoiler.

Special Vehicle Engineering

Rod Mansfield was an early AVO member, and was also responsible for setting up Ford's Special Vehicle Engineering department in 1980.

At AVO from 1970, Mansfield worked for Bob Howe (see page 26), replaced Henry Taylor in 1972, and later engineered all AVO products until that project closed in 1975. After five years in relative obscurity, he was suddenly asked to set up Special Vehicle Engineering.

SVE's brief was to develop cars that were more sporty, and more specialized than those normally covered by Ford's engineering team. Like AVO before it, SVE was really a team within a team, though liaison with all other departments was maintained.

SVE's first successful projects were the Capri 2.8i and the original Fiesta XR2, these being followed by the original Escort XR3i and the Sierra XR4×4. Although SVE then worked on finalizing the still-born RS1700T, the next to go on sale (in 1984) was the first-generation fuel-injected Escort RS Turbo.

Other cars like the Escort Cabriolet and the Sierra RS Cosworth were also important SVE projects, but serious work on the Escort RS Cosworth was a vital responsibility after 1989, and included several little-publicized 'why-don't-we...?' dabbles with rear-drive Escorts, some driven by Cosworth (Scorpio-type) 24-valve V6 engines.

Mansfield himself then enjoyed a colourful 1990s, which included spells at Aston Martin, setting up an SVE-like operation at Ford-USA, and even spending time as managing director of Lotus. SVE developed strongly without him, and he worked on every fast and special Ford that the company announced thereafter, though surprisingly little on the 2ltr/16-valve Escort RS2000.

activity. I would argue that this was really the beginning of what became Special Vehicle Engineering (SVE) ...

And from SVE, came Escort RS models of the 1980s and 1990s.

THREE NEW RS MODELS

Three rather different RS Escorts evolved in 1974 and 1975, each with its own character. Put yourself in the mind of the Escort enthusiast of the mid-1970s, and see how Ford had stirred its product mix.

How should you choose between the Escort RS1800 or the Escort RS Mexico which stemmed from the same base, at the same time? Then consider the RS2000 itself – almost as powerful as the RS1800 but mechanically simpler, and with unique front-end styling.

Twin-cam, 16-valve 'homologation special' or single-cam road cars? Top of the Mk II RS range, the 'executive version', or the 'entry-level' model? Finicky and difficult to maintain, or work-a-day sports saloon?

At this point I should side-line the RS2000 Mk II, and concentrate on the other types. Although they were very similar (much closer together, in many ways, than either of them to the RS2000 Mk II), their characters and performance were quite different. Yet they were built in the same period, designed and developed by the same small teams. RS1800s, in fact, were price-listed from mid-1975 to late 1977, and RS Mexicos from January 1976 to the summer of 1978. After that the RS2000 Mk II held the line, on its own – and sold best of all.

Years later, though, their reputations are completely different. Compared with the RS2000 Mk II, and the charismatic

All RS2000 Mk IIs were built with a four-headlamp nose, though the cast alloy wheels did not feature on 'Base' models built after 1978.

This was the 1979 Model Year RS2000, complete with specification-enhancing tinted window glass.

RS1800, the RS Mexico is almost forgotten. The RS1800, on the other, will be famous, valuable and fabulous (yes – look up the traditional dictionary definition if you don't know what I mean ...) for a long time to come.

It is the RS1800s that usually cause most interest at big Ford one-make events, for they are rare, and not often seen in standard, preserved form. Which brings me to Deep Breath time! At this point I suppose I must talk about numbers.

Not 'How fast?', or 'How much will they cost?' but, in this case: 'How many were built?'

The fact is that Escort RS Mexicos, and particularly Escort RS1800 road cars, were rather rare – and today their numbers have fallen still further.

Whenever specialist Ford authors talk to groups of RS enthusiasts we can guarantee to be asked similar questions, because Ford has always been extraordinarily secretive

about the number of Escort RS cars ever built.

Why? One reason, I am sure, is that some of the cars were homologated suspiciously quickly, and even today an admission of the actual figures built might be embarrassing. Another is that later cars were assembled, or part-assembled in the case of the RS1800, at Saarlouis in West Germany, where individual facts and figures are difficult to pin-point – and where RS1800s were actually programmed as RS Mexicos to start with! A third is that Ford is a company that hates looking back, would rather not keep any records that are not absolutely vital, and would rather leave Ford enthusiasts like you and I in blissful ignorance.

I'm grateful to Jeremy Walton, therefore, for showing me figures for UK-market sales, which tell us a lot. From 1976 to 1979, 2,290 RS Mexicos were delivered to British customers (a few of them may have been left-over

Mk Is), but in the same period there were only 109 RS1800s. Compare either of those figures with 10,039 UK-market RS2000 Mk IIs, and you'll see why they are real rarities.

DEVELOPMENT AND EVOLUTION

Work on new-generation Escort RSs began in 1973–74, but the decision to close down the special AVO factory put back their launch by several months. In addition, because of the launch of the mainstream Escort 1600 Sport of 1975, no-one outside Ford and its dealers was expecting a Pinto-engined RS Mexico at all when that car was finally launched in January 1976!

The mainstream Mk II Escort range was introduced in January 1975, and although a mock-up rally car was shown (and photographed) at that time, the very first hand-built RS1800s were not delivered until the middle of that year, and the RS Mexico did not go on sale until January 1976.

Instead of the original Mexico–RS2000–RS1600 range, this time there would be a more advanced and up-market listing – of RS Mexico–RS2000–RS1800. In every case the second-generation cars would be very different from their ancestors. Drawing from the experience of the Mk Is, and their record, the two most important decisions imposed on AVO (following an exhaustive financial and commercial analysis) were that the cars would have to be manufactured in Germany, among the mainstream Escorts at Saarlouis – and that the RS1800 would only be made in tiny numbers.

RS2000s were also marketed successfully in Australia, where no fewer than 2,400 were sold. These unique-to-Oz sports wheels were an option – as was a four-door style. Four doors? Oh yes – I have actually seen one of them, 'Down Under'.

Escort RS1800 (1975–1978)

Layout
Unit construction steel body/chassis structure. Two-door, front engine/rear drive, sold as four-seater sports saloon.

Engine
Type	Ford-Cosworth BDA
Block material	Cast aluminium
Head material	Cast aluminium
Cylinders	4 in-line
Cooling	Water
Bore and stroke	86.75 × 77.62mm
Capacity	1,835cc
Main bearings	5
Valves	4 per cylinder, directly operated by twin overhead camshafts and inverted bucket-type tappets, with camshafts driven by cogged belt from the crankshaft
Compression ratio	10.0:1
Carburettors	One downdraught dual-choke Weber Type 32/36 DGAV
Max power	115bhp @ 6,000rpm
Max torque	120lb ft at 4,000rpm

Transmission
Four-speed manual gearbox, all-synchromesh
Clutch	Single plate, diaphragm spring

Overall gearbox ratios
Top	3.54
3rd	4.46
2nd	6.41
1st	11.89
Reverse	11.93
Final drive	3.54:1 (Hypoid Bevel)

(18.5mph (29.8km/h)/1,000rpm in top gear)

Suspension and steering
Front	Independent, by coil springs, MacPherson struts, track control arms, and anti-roll bar
Rear	Live (beam) axle, with half-elliptic leaf springs, radius arms and telescopic dampers
Steering	Rack-and-pinion
Tyres	175/70HR-13in radial-ply
Wheels	Steel disc, bolt-on fixing
Rim width	5.5in

Escort RS Mexico (1976–1978)

Layout
Unit construction steel body/chassis structure. Two-door, front engine/rear drive, sold as four-seater sports saloon.

Engine

Type	Ford 'Pinto'
Block material	Cast iron
Head material	Cast iron
Cylinders	4 in-line
Cooling	Water
Bore and stroke	87.5×66.0mm
Capacity	1,593cc
Main bearings	5
Valves	2 per cylinder, directly operated by single overhead camshaft and inverted bucket-type tappets, via steel fingers, with the camshaft driven by cogged belt from the crankshaft
Compression ratio	9.2:1
Carburettors	One downdraught dual-choke Weber Type 32/36 DGAV
Max power	95bhp @ 5,750rpm
Max torque	92lb ft at 4,000rpm

Transmission
Four-speed manual gearbox, all-synchromesh

Clutch	Single plate, diaphragm spring

Overall gearbox ratios

Top	3.54
3rd	4.85
2nd	6.97
1st	12.92
Reverse	12.96
Final drive	3.54:1 (Hypoid Bevel)

(18.7mph(30.1km/h)/1,000rpm in top gear)

Suspension and steering

Front	Independent, by coil springs, MacPherson struts, track control arms, and anti-roll bar
Rear	Live (beam) axle, with half-elliptic leaf springs, radius arms and telescopic dampers
Steering	Rack-and-pinion
Tyres	175/70HR-13in radial-ply
Wheels	Cast alloy disc, bolt-on fixing
Rim width	6.0in

Brakes

Type	Disc brakes at front, drums at rear, hydraulically operated
Size	9.62in front discs, 9.0×1.75in rear drums

Escort RS Mexico (1976–1978) *continued*

Dimensions (in/mm)

Track	
Front	51.7/1,310
Rear	52.0/1,320
Wheelbase	94.5/2,400
Overall length	156.6/3,980
Overall width	60.5/1,540
Overall height	55.5/1,410
Unladen weight	1,990lb/902kg

UK retail price

At launch in 1976	£2,443

This studio shot confirms the GL badge. But, if the 110bhp engine could be fitted, how important was the badge? Four-door types were available, too.

BADGING AND TRIM

Externally, the RS Mexico looked very much like the 1600 Sport except for the use of the moulded front spoiler under the front bumper, which is to say that it had front quarter bumpers, and '1.6' badges behind the front wheel arches, along with the same pin-striping along the flanks. The 'Mexico' decal appeared on the rear quarters in place of the 1600 Sport's own badges. Road wheels seen on these cars – sculptured steel or cast alloys – were the same as those used on Escort RS2000 Mk IIs or RS1800s.

Production-type RS1800s looked very similar to RS Mexicos (same shell, same grille, same proportions), though they had special '1.8' badges on the front wings, a single, broad, two-tone blue stripe on the flanks at wheelarch-top level, and 'RS1800' decals on the rear quarters and on the boot lid, along with a black-painted panel across the tail.

Although there was only one RS Mexico trim specification (this was virtually shared with the 'basic' RS1800 trim) there were two types of RS1800. The RS1800 'base' and RS Mexico cars were fitted out rather like the Escort 1600 Sport of the day. On the other hand, the more expensive RS1800 'Custom' had superb contoured/reclinable front seats, a centre console with provision for a radio mounting, a fascia-mounted clock, and the extra fascia/instrument equipment normally found in RS2000 Mk IIs of the day.

Because very few people ordered RS1800s for pure road use, there was little demand for the 'Custom' pack, so this was dropped at the end of 1976. The road-car users, I assume, had also tried the alternative of an RS2000 Mk II, and usually opted for that instead.

As road cars, at the time both were rather overshadowed by the all-round excellence of the RS2000 Mk II, but in later years their own distinctive character were recognized.

Today's values, I believe, reflect their worth – the RS1800 in particular being a rare and ultra-desirable beast.

Not forgetting that price inflation was raging at this time, at launch in mid-1975 the RS1800 was priced at £2,416 ('Basic' trim), or £2,527 ('Custom' trim). When the RS Mexico appeared in January 1976, it retailed for £2,443.

The last published price for the RS1800 (late 1977) was £4,275, and when the last of the RS Mexicos was made in the autumn of 1978 it was listed at £3,632.

Because I was always surprised that it did not sell as well as expected, let me now put in a final word for the RS Mexico. It is a fast car which handles equally as well as the other Mk II RS models, yet does not suffer from any of the parts supply problems of the other types. Doesn't that make it worth considering, today?

RS2000 Mk II style, in this composite shot – seats, fascia, wheels and up-market door furniture. No wonder the RS2000 became an RS best-seller.

Ford Escort Performance

Mark II models

This is a summary of the figures achieved by Britain's most authoritative magazine, *Autocar*, of cars supplied for test by Ford over the years:

Model	Escort RS1800 1,835cc 115bhp	Escort RS2000 1,993cc 110bhp	Escort RS Mexico* 1,593cc 95bhp
Max speed (mph)	111	109	106 (claimed)
Accn (sec):			
0–60mph	9.0	8.6	11.1
0–80mph	16.6	16.9	23.0
0–100mph	32.9	33.6	–
Standing ¼-mile (sec)	16.9	16.7	17.8
Consumption (mpg)			
Overall	26.5	24.7	27.2
Typical	28	28	30
Kerb weight (lb/kg)	2,016/914	2,075/941	1,999/903
Year tested:	1975	1976	1976

* Tested by *Motor Sport*

This useful centre console was fitted to the RS2000 Mk II.

The RS Mexico Mk II of 1976–78 used a 95bhp 1.6ltr Pinto engine, enough to produce a top speed of more than 100mph (160km/h). The registration number of this launch car is consecutive with the first batch of Boreham's 'works' RS1800s of 1975!

this a car that many owners used for long journeys, and for business.

Because the RS Mexico was dropped in 1978, this left the RS2000 on its own. Though no mechanical changes were ever made, Ford then decided to split it into two derivatives, effective September 1978. For the rest of its production life, therefore, there were two RS2000 Mk IIs, the RS2000 'base' model, and the RS2000 Custom.

The base model was always considerably cheaper than the Custom – £3,902 compared with £4,416 at first – a saving signposted by

it having normal '(low-back, Sport-type) instead of sports-type reclining seats, and pressed-steel instead of cast alloy road wheels. For 1979 the RS2000 Custom got a new type of wrap-around sports seat, along with bronze-tinted glass, and a remote-adjustable driver's mirror.

Once again, Ford miscalculated. Apparently they thought that those wanting a car to prepare for motorsport would flock to buy 'base' models – but they didn't. The 'Custom' type always outsold the 'base' model by at least four to one.

Each and every European-built production car was a two-door saloon, though four-door models, complete with beaky noses and every other authentic detail, were assembled in small numbers in Australia. Production at Saarlouis ran down during 1980, and along with all other rear-drive Escorts finally ended in July of that year, when the 'base' car was priced at £4,995, the Custom at £5,650.

Thereafter the entire factory was converted to build new-generation front-wheel-drive Escorts, and for a time at least the 'RS' badge went into limbo. According to the most authoritative, but only semi-official, sources, we now know that no fewer than 25,638 RS2000 Mk IIs were produced at Saarlouis, of which 10,039 were delivered to British customers.

RS2000 DOWN UNDER

When it comes to defining Ford models, never say 'Never'! Somewhere, somehow, there was usually an exception to prove the rules, which explains why I have personally seen flat-nosed Escort RS2000 Mk IIs, and four-door RS2000 Mk IIs – both of them in Australia!

Between 1970 and 1981, Ford-Australia built 146,849 rear-drive Escorts, most of them from sets and panel kits provided from Dagenham. Not even counting their special model names, or their colour schemes, they differed significantly from those sold in Europe.

In 1977 Ford-Australia announced a 93bhp version of the 2ltr Pinto-engined Escort Mk II, calling it a GL or a Ghia, depending on the trim pack. Compared with the RS2000 Mk II, the power reduction was caused by the harsh exhaust emission regulations which were being imposed.

A 'Rally pack' was soon added as an equipment option. All these cars were in conventional, flat-nose trim, and for 1979 and 1980 they also came with rectangular headlamps (which never featured on any European RS Escorts). Rally Pack cars received a dress-up kit, which included most of the RS gizmos (including a flat steering wheel, a rev counter, a rear spoiler and special wheels which might look familiar to RS2000 owners), along with a sporty suspension pack and (blissful in the hot Oz climate) air conditioning as optional extras.

But no 'RS' model for the time being, and no radius arms for the rear suspension.

Because these cars were built in their thousands, it was from these cars that John Griffiths based his application for the homologation of the flat-nose RS2000, cars which were used widely in motorsport for the next decade and more.

Now for the confusion. Having imported just twenty-five genuine beaky-nose RS2000 Mk IIs from Saarlouis in 1976–77, Ford-Australia then decided to do its own thing. In 1979 and 1980 they arranged to produce 93bhp RS2000s from imported kits – the immediate difference being that these cars had standard Australia-spec suspension (which was not the same as the Walkinshaw-refined RS type), did not have rear radius arms, and used different road wheels.

But – and you're not going to find this easy to accept – not only were these cars available as two-door or four-door types, but there was also an automatic transmission option!

Confused? When I saw these cars on a visit to Australia in the 1990s, I certainly was, and when I then discovered that the 2ltr Escorts assembled by similar methods in South Africa differed yet again, I realized that the historian's job is awesomely difficult!

Roger Clark (ahead – just) and Gerry Marshall won the 1974 Tour of Britain in these RS2000 sister cars. On the circuits they were rarely further apart than this.

Except in the UK, where Roger Clark was still king, this time with his Cossack-liveried cars, and in Europe (where Gilbert Staepelaere won several events in his self-prepared cars), there was only one major victory to report – in the Lombard-RAC rally, where Timo Makinen notched up his hat-trick (and the Escort its four-in-four sequence).

The need to improve soon resulted in ex-AVO engineer (and saloon car racer) Allan Wilkinson joining the team as a dedicated rally engineer, and a lot more development work was done on the cars. Even so, expeditions to Morocco and the Australian Southern Cross were embarrassing failures, though an unexpected victory in South Africa (the Total rally) was a nice bonus.

For almost every Escort fanatic, though, the most exciting win of all came at the end of the 1976 year, when Roger Clark won the RAC in his Cossack-liveried car, having fought an event-long battle with Pentti Airikkala in one of David Sutton's cars. Bjorn Waldegard, new to the team, with little Escort experience, took third place.

Though David Sutton's 'works-replica' machines were excellent at this time, they now became obsolete soon after they were built, simply because Boreham had begun to introduce so many innovations.

In four years, between 1976 and 1979, the RS1800 was gradually turned into a worthy World Champion. Not only could it win in Britain and Scandinavia, but 'works' cars also started winning impressively in the Safari, Portugal, New Zealand, North America, South Africa and Greece.

To do this there was more power (sometimes up to 272bhp with fuel injection), more sophisticated suspension (reaction struts at the front for tarmac events, coil springs instead of leaf springs at the rear), rear axle oil coolers, and more favourable weight distribution. Egged on by John Taylor in particular, Dunlop produced better tyres, the intriguing A2 casing (part racer, part rallycross in its inspiration) being one result.

Along the way the 'works' team attracted Bjorn Waldegard from Lancia, to drive alongside Hannu Mikkola, who had rejoined, and they also uncovered a sparkling new talent in Ari Vatanen. With Roger Clark still at his peak, Boreham really had too many drivers, but this was

What a way for the 'works' RS1600 to end its rallying career – by Timo Makinen winning the RAC rally of 1974. It was Timo's second straight win, the Escort's third.

riches they were happy to hoard, and to exploit.

From 1977, incidentally, to evade the latest homologation restrictions, the RS1800 was craftily re-homologated as the 'Escort RS', officially as a different type of Escort, but one which ensured that all the 16-valve rally cars could now routinely have 2ltr engines, five-speed boxes, Atlas axles and four-wheel disc brakes, instead of using them as evolutionary items!

The build-up to taking World Championship honours took time, though it might have been achieved in 1977 or in 1978. In 1977 the honours finally went to Fiat – though the Escorts nevertheless won handsomely in the Safari (the wettest Safari on record), Greece (rough, tough and hot) and the RAC (Bjorn Waldegard was the winning driver in each case).

For 1978, with Hannu Mikkola back on board, they might also have done the trick, except that Fiat's 131 Abarth saloons had become truly formidable, and from September their season was stunted by a long factory pay strike. The Escort's qualities, though, were never more easily demonstrated when no fewer than six 'private entries' started the RAC rally (it was amazing how 'un-private' some of them actually were ...).

Not only did Hannu Mikkola's car (built and run by David Sutton) win the event (it was his first, but the Escort's seventh), but Bjorn Waldegard was second, Russell Brookes third and John Taylor seventh. Not bad for an effort where Peter Ashcroft and co-ordinator Charles Reynolds both officially stayed away.

Then came 1979, the year in which Ford won the World Rally Championship for Makes, while two team drivers – Bjorn Waldegard and Hannu Mikkola – topped the Drivers' category. For the factory cars, the statistics tell their own story – nine starts, five victories (Portugal, Acropolis, New Zealand, Quebec and RAC rally), five second places and three thirds. On the other hand these figures don't tell us that Waldegard would also have won the Monte if his

The Rothmans Escorts

Between 1979 and the end of 1981 (when Ari Vatanen won the World Rally Championship for Drivers), the 'Rothmans Escorts' were the most famous of all these types. In 1979 they were usually prepared at Boreham, but in 1980 and 1981 they were always based in London, where David Sutton (Cars) ran a works-blessed operation.

In 1979 'works' Escorts with the original Rothmans livery started eleven times, notching up victory in the Acropolis, Quebec (Canada) and Cyprus rallies, along with podium places in the 1,000 Lakes, New Zealand and Quebec.

The 1979 cars carried these identities:

POO 504R	POO 505R
STW 201R	WTW 567S
FEV 1T	GVX 488T
IZ8320 (New Zealand registration)	

In 1980 and 1981, this time with the definitive red/gold/blue and white livery, the cars carried out a complex programme. In 1980, outright victories came in the Acropolis, Cyprus and Welsh rallies, while in 1981 victories came in the Acropolis, Brazil, Mintex (Britain), 1,000 Lakes and Welsh events.

In these years, cars to carry the Rothmans/David Sutton livery were as follows:

MLD 999P	MTW 200P (only used as practice and publicity car)	
STW 201R	UYY 256S	
CLM 184T	DKP 191T	
GVX 489T	EUC 958V	
EUW 938V	EUW 939V	
PLY 929W	RRK 425W	VLE 756X

Even in the year 2000, the last car (VLE 756X) was still preserved at the National Motor Museum, Beaulieu, Hampshire. All other cars were sold off, and most soon lost their distinctive livery.

Roger Clark, Escort RS1800, and Cossack sponsorship – an unforgettable combination in 1975 and 1976. Here they are on their way to winning the Scottish rally of 1975.

way had not been sabotaged by rocks placed in the road on a late special stage.

That was the year in which the most special Escorts of all time – three near-mythical 'tarmac specials' – were built. On the Monte, and on tarmac in Ireland, had you ever seen RSs with such wide wheelarches before? Or with their engines so low, and so far back into the bulkhead? Have you ever seen Escorts which handled so well on tarmac, or were so reliable *everywhere*?

AFTERLIFE

Even though the 'works' team retired from rallying at the of 1979 (to develop the RS1700T – *see* Chapter 6), the rear-drive Escort was not finished as a world force in rallying, as Rothmans, the cigarette company, together with the David Sutton team, soon proved.

With Ari Vatanen as their favoured driver, and with backing from Boreham, the Sutton/Rothmans team built a fleet of new RSs to compete all round the world. The strategy was sound – David Sutton didn't need super-modern engineering, merely super-competitive works-backed machines which could match the rest of the world.

In 1980, the first season, from a standing start, success for the Acton-based team was limited – if, that is, you call a win in the Acropolis and two other second places in World Championship events as 'limited' – but in 1981 there was to be an all-out assault on the World Championship.

Ari Vatanen, backed up on occasion by Pentti Airikkala and Malcolm Wilson, started twelve rallies, won three World Championship rounds (Acropolis, Brazil and 1000 Lakes) and eventually won the World Drivers' Championship, using obsolete Escort RSs – and a full year after the rear-drive cars had finally gone out of production.

Complete with its square-arch, Zakspeed-style body kit, Roger Clark's Escort RS1800 on its way to fifth place in the 1976 Monte.

After Rothmans had taken their money off to another manufacturer – Opel – this was surely the end for the famous rear-drive Escorts? Well, yes and no ... There were to be no more World Championship successes, though Vatanen took second in Sweden in 1982 – and even in 1984, its final year as an homologated car, the Escort RS won four European Championship rallies.

By the mid-1980s the rear-drive Escort could still win at British national level – as Louise Aitken-Walker once memorably demonstrated – but once the four-wheel-drive Supercars began to appear it was finally overwhelmed. Even then it was not the end for the car, for when the RAC MSA started issuing historic rally car 'log books' at the beginning of the 1990s it discovered that the majority of British rally cars were Escorts!

This, in summary, is the Escort's record in fourteen glorious years:

Major rally wins – 'works' and 'works-assisted' cars – 1968–81

1968 Tulip, Austrian Alpine, Acropolis and 1,000 Lakes

1969 Tulip, Austrian Alpine and 1,000 Lakes

1970 World Cup (London–Mexico) and 1,000 Lakes

1971 Cyprus

1972 Safari and RAC

1973 New Zealand, 1,000 Lakes and RAC

1974 Tour of Britain, 1,000 Lakes and RAC

1975 RAC

1976 Tour of Britain, Total (South Africa) and RAC

1977 Safari, Acropolis, 1,000 Lakes and RAC

1978 Cyprus and RAC

Timo Makinen and Henry Liddon used MTW 200P to win the South African Total rally in 1976.

1979 Portugal, Acropolis, New Zealand, Quebec (Canada), Cyprus and RAC

1980 Acropolis and Cyprus

1981 Acropolis, Brazil and 1,000 Lakes

Alan Mann

Originally a car salesman, then an amateur racing driver, Alan Mann next owned his own garage in Sussex, and eventually ran a Ford dealership near Brighton – yet he moved into team management almost by accident.

First he persuaded Ford to back his efforts in Cortinas. Success in the 1963 British Touring Car Championship and a chance meeting with John Holman (of the USA's famous Holman & Moody preparation outfit) then allowed him to set up Alan Mann Racing (*see* page 96), which dominated the saloon car racing scene until the end of the decade. Drifting away from Ford at the end of 1969 ('Stuart Turner didn't like motor racing, and he didn't like me ...'), he abandoned motor racing, developed his strong interest in helicopters, bought Fairoaks airfield in Surrey, and by the end of the century was about as far removed from Escort RS cars as he could possibly be.

In the meantime, the Escort built a great race-track reputation. Mainly backed by the factories – Britain *and* Germany – but sometimes in private ownership, these cars were quite outstanding.

In 1968 Ford planned an assault on the British *and* European Saloon Car Championships. Because Boreham did not plan to run its own cars, Broadspeed was invited to

Ari Vatanen easily won the 1976 Tour of Britain in this Group 1 RS2000 Mk II.

run 1300GTs, and Alan Mann Racing ran Twin-Cams.

PUSHROD RACERS

Broadspeed's 'Kent'-engined cars had TJ injection, producing 145bhp at 9,000rpm, using much-modified cast-iron heads into which Ralph Broad had inserted down-draught inlet ports: they were supreme class winners, but not reliable, with John Fitzpatrick and Chris Craft driving the cars.

There was even time to send cars into Europe where Chris Craft and rally-driver Roger Clark easily won their capacity class in the Nurburgring Six-Hour race. In 1969, the Broadspeed Escorts were so fast that they won their British class nine times.

In 1970 Fitzpatrick once again ran a pushrod 1300GT, and it was another emphatic Championship year, because Chris Craft won his class six times in a Twin-Cam, and Fitzpatrick won seven times in the 1300GT. Late in the season the 1300GT (EVX 256H) was re-engined as

---

Alan Mann Racing

Founded in 1964, and closed down at the end of 1969, AMR of Byfleet was probably the most successful saloon-car race-preparation team of the decade. Before then, Mann (*see* page 95) had already started running Cortina GTs, and had prepared the Ford Falcons which so nearly won the 1964 Monte Carlo Rally.

AMR's first Ford contract was to run Lotus-Cortinas in the European Touring Car Championship (where they had five outright victories) to which the running of the Ford Mustangs in the Tour de France (which they won) was soon added.

In 1965, not only did Sir John Whitmore's AMR-prepared Lotus-Cortina win the 1965 ETC Championship, but their team of AC Daytona Cobras also won the World Sports Car Championship. A contract to build lightweight GT40s was not progressed far, building film cars including 'Chitty Chitty Bang Bang' was fun, as was the development of the ex-Monte Falcons for saloon car racing, where they swept all before them.

AMR then prepared the new Escort Twin-Cams for the British and the European Saloon Car Championships, where Frank Gardner won the British in 1968, and performed well in the European. In 1969 Gardner's car won several British events outright.

At the end of 1969, with Alan Mann no longer in favour at Boreham, and with Frank Gardner anxious to develop his own team, Alan Mann sold out to Gardner, closed down AMR, and walked away from the sport.

(Above) *For more than four years, the AVO factory in Essex was the home of the Escort RS range. RS1600s and Mexicos share space here, in 1971.*

Squat stance, fat tyres, negative front camber and no surplus decoration – this early example was typical of the new breed of Escort RS models at the time.

(Below) *The Mexico was developed in a matter of months, immediately after the famous Daily Mirror World Cup rally victory. It was on sale from 1970 to 1974.*

Rare bird! This is a carefully preserved RS1800 road car, of which only 109 were originally registered in the UK. Most RS1800s were used in motorsport.

(Below) The RS Mexico of 1976–78 was the simplest and least expensive of the three-car Mk II range.

(Above) The Cosworth-designed 16-valve BDA engine was the most famous RS 'building block' of all. Originally with an iron block, but here with an aluminium block, it has powered thousands of famous race and rally winners since 1970.

Always intended to be the most versatile of the late-1970s Escort RS range, the 'beaky-nose' RS2000 sold very well, with more than 20,000 being built in five years.

Styling guru Jack Telnack was challenged to make the late-1970s RS2000 look different from its relatives – and with this four-headlamp nose he certainly succeeded.

(Right) Count the styling 'cues' which make this late-1970s RS2000 unmistakeable: unique front-end style, four-spoke alloys and badge transfers.

Celebrations in Mexico at the end of the World Cup Rally of 1970. The winning car (FEV 1H) is on the left of the picture. Crew members (left to right) are: Rauno Aaltonen, Henry Liddon, Gunnar Palm, Hannu Mikkola, Gilbert Staepelaere and Timo Makinen.

A well-known picture of a sensational victory – Ford's first Safari victory, of 1972, with Hannu Mikkola and Gunnar Palm as the winning crew.

(Below) Who will ever forget the way that Roger Clark and co-driver Stuart Pegg won the RAC rally of 1976, in the legendary Cossack-liveried RS1800, POO 505R?

(Bottom) Ford sent a team of brand-new RS1800s to tackle the Safari in 1977. Bjorn Waldegard won the event in STW 201R – and this is Vic 'Junior' Preston's sister car, STW 203R. (Picture: Reinhard Klein)

a Twin-Cam and won the Motor Show 200 outright.

For 1971, Broadspeed put Dave Matthews into a 1300GT, selling off John Fitzpatrick's old car to Vince Woodman, those cars dominating the class. In 1972 Woodman had a new Broadspeed-built 1300GT, but this was the end for the pushrod-engined cars, as new FIA Group 2 regulations then allowed alternative cylinder heads.

TREMENDOUS TWIN-CAMS

Because the regulations, home and abroad, were very different – Group 5 at home, Group 2 abroad – there were two Alan Mann Racing programmes in 1968. With Len Bailey as engineer, these were the first

Escorts to have coil–spring rear suspension.

The 'British' Twin-Cams used 1.6ltr/210bhp 16-valve Cosworth FVA F2 engines, but in Europe AMR used a 1,594cc version of the 'standard' Lotus-Ford power unit, Vegan-tune-tuned, with 170–180bhp.

Though Twin-Cams did not race until May 1968, Gardner easily won the British series with the famous XO0 349F – winning his class eight times: in two races he also won outright. The European effort was not as successful. Because the car had 30bhp less, it could not always defeat the Alfa Romeos and BMWs. Even so, this 8-valve car won its debut race (at Zolder, in Belgium).

In 1969 AMR concentrated on the British series. New rules meant that Gardner had to run with an 8-valve Lotus-Ford engine that pushed out around 185bhp. Throughout the

Bjorn Waldegard won the 1977 East African Safari in STW 201R. It was one of the wettest Safaris on record.

Ford Escort – major motorsport victories from 1968

1968

World Rally Championship for Makes		
British Touring Car Championship		
Tulip rally	Roger Clark	Escort Twin-Cam
Austrian Alpine rally	Bengt Soderstrom	Escort Twin-Cam
Acropolis rally	Roger Clark	Escort Twin-Cam
1,000 Lakes rally	Hannu Mikkola	Escort Twin-Cam
British Rally Championship	2 victories	Escort Twin-Cam
Zolder race, Belgium	Frank Gardner	Escort Twin-Cam
(European Touring Car Championship)		

1969

World Rally Championship for Makes		
Tulip rally	Gilbert Staepelaere	Escort Twin-Cam
Austrian Alpine rally	Hannu Mikkola	Escort Twin-Cam
1,000 Lakes rally	Hannu Mikkola	Escort Twin-Cam
British Rally Championship	2 victories	Escort Twin-Cam

1970

World Cup Rally		
(London–Mexico)	Hannu Mikkola	Escort Mexico (prototype)
1,000 Lakes rally	Hannu Mikkola	Escort Twin-Cam
British Rally Championship	1 victory	

1971

Jarama race, Spain (European		
Touring Car Championship)	John Fitzpatrick/	
	Jochen Mass	Escort RS1600

1972

Hong Kong rally	Timo Makinen	Escort RS1600
East African Safari rally	Hannu Mikkola	Escort RS1600
RAC rally	Roger Clark	Escort RS1600
British Rally Championship	3 victories	

1973

New Zealand rally	Hannu Mikkola	Escort RS1600
1,000 Lakes rally	Timo Makinen	Escort RS1600
RAC rally	Timo Makinen	Escort RS1600
European Rallycross Championship	John Taylor	Escort RS1600
British Rally Championship	2 victories	

1974

Tour of Britain	Roger Clark	Escort RS2000
1,000 Lakes	Hannu Mikkola	Escort RS1600
RAC rally	Timo Makinen	Escort RS1600

1974 continued
Nurburgring, Germany   Hans Heyer/
(European Touring Car Championship)   Klaus Ludwig   Escort RS1600
British Rally Championship   1 victory

1975
Tour of Britain   Tony Pond   Escort RS2000
RAC rally   Timo Makinen   Escort RS1800
Kyalami, South Africa, 12-Hour race   Hans Heyer/
                                             H Hennige   Escort RS1800
British Rally Championship   4 victories

1976
Tour of Britain   Ari Vatanen   Escort RS2000
Total (South Africa) rally   Timo Makinen   Escort RS1800
RAC rally   Roger Clark   Escort RS1800
British Rally Championship   4 victories

1977
East African Safari rally   Bjorn Waldegard   Escort RS1800
Acropolis rally   Bjorn Waldegard   Escort RS1800
1,000 Lakes rally   Kyosti Hamalainen   Escort RS1800
RAC rally   Bjorn Waldegard   Escort RS1800
British Rally Championship   1 victory

1978
Swedish rally   Bjorn Waldegard   Escort RS1800
RAC rally   Hannu Mikkola   Escort RS1800
European Rallycross Championship   Martin Schanche   Escort RS1800
British Rally Championship   3 victories

1979
World Rally Championship for Makes
World Rally Championship, Drivers   (Bjorn Waldegard)
Portugal rally   Hannu Mikkola   Escort RS1800
Acropolis rally   Bjorn Waldegard   Escort RS1800
New Zealand rally   Hannu Mikkola   Escort RS1800
Quebec (Canadian) rally   Bjorn Waldegard   Escort RS1800
RAC rally   Hannu Mikkola   Escort RS1800
European Rallycross Championship   Martin Schanche   Escort RS1800
British Rally Championship   3 victories

1980
Acropolis rally   Ari Vatanen   Escort RS1800
British Rally Championship   3 victories

Ford Escort – major motorsport victories from 1968 *continued*

1981
World Rally Championship, Drivers	(Ari Vatanen)	
Acropolis rally	Ari Vatanen	Escort RS1800
Brazil rally	Ari Vatanen	Escort RS1800
1,000 Lakes rally	Ari Vatanen	Escort RS1800
European Rallycross Championship	Martin Schanche	Escort RS1800
British Rally Championship	2 victories	

1984
European Rallycross Championship	Martin Schanche	Escort XR3 4×4

1986
British Touring Car Championship (second)	Richard Longman	Escort RS Turbo

1993
Portugal rally	François Delecour	Escort RS Cosworth
Tour de Corse (Corsica) rally	François Delecour	Escort RS Cosworth
Acropolis rally	Miki Biasion	Escort RS Cosworth
San Remo rally	Gianfranco Cunico	Escort RS Cosworth
Spanish rally	François Delecour	Escort RS Cosworth
European Rally Championship	15 victories	Escort RS Cosworth
British Rally Championship	1 victory	Escort RS Cosworth

1994
Monte Carlo rally	François Delecour	Escort RS Cosworth
1,000 Lakes rally	Tommi Makinen	Escort RS Cosworth
European Rally Championship	28 victories	Escort RS Cosworth
British Rally Championship	5 victories	Escort RS Cosworth

1995
European Rally Championship	25 victories	Escort RS Cosworth
European Rallycross Championship	Martin Schanche	Escort RS2000 4×4
British Rally Championship	3 victories	Escort RS Cosworth

1996
Monte Carlo rally	Patrick Bernardini	Escort RS Cosworth
Indonesia rally	Carlos Sainz	Escort RS Cosworth
European Rally Championship	24 victories	Escort RS Cosworth
British Rally Championship	2 victories	Escort RS Cosworth

1997
Acropolis rally	Carlos Sainz	Escort World Rally Car
Indonesia rally	Carlos Sainz	Escort World Rally Car
European Rally Championship	7 victories	Escort RS Cosworth
	6 victories	Escort World Rally Car
European Rallycross Championship	Ludvig Hunsbedt	Escort RS2000 4×4

1998		
European Rally Championship	8 victories	Escort RS Cosworth
	6 victories	Escort WRC
1999		
European Rally Championship	2 victories	Escort RS Cosworth
	2 victories	Escort WRC

year it ran with a 'supercharged' power unit (a rather ludicrous, but regulation-cracking, heater blower fan was fitted upstream of the inlet trumpets), still won three races outright, and finished third in the Championship.

Alan Mann then pulled out of motor sport. Even so, in 1970 no fewer than twenty-four Group 2 Twin-Cams raced in the BRSCC British Championship – in the 2ltr class no other car got a look-in. Broadspeed's Chris Craft set the pace, driving a 177bhp/TJ-injected car, this superbly prepared car was the pace setter.

8 VALVES GOOD, 16 VALVES BETTER ...

For 1971, Broadspeed built an RS1600, with a Lucas-injected 240bhp/1.7ltr engine. Fitzpatrick started by beating all comers, but had an eventful year including a written-off car, a series of podium finishes, and another outright win at Brands Hatch in September. Then came the Brands Hatch Motor Show 200 meeting – Frank Gardner's Camaro suffered a tyre burst, veered into the Escort, nudged it into multiple rolls, and wrote it off again! Even so, Fitzpatrick had won the 2ltr class in the series, winning seven times in twelve events.

For 1972 Broadspeed built a 265bhp/1.8ltr RS1600 for Dave Matthews while Boreham

built a car which Gerry Birrell occasionally drove. In a ten-round series, Matthews won his 2ltr class seven times: towards the end of the season Tom Walkinshaw's and Dave Brodie's cars also showed well.

In 1973 the Saloon Car Championship sagged badly, mainly because for 1974 the only eligible cars would be Group 1 machines: this, by definition, would ban the 16-valve Escorts.

Although the series was dominated by Gardner's Chevrolet Camaro, the RS1600s were always 'best of the rest'. One or other of the cars finished second overall in four races and third overall five times. As expected, Andy Rouse was the most successful individual driver.

For 1973, Ford took advantage of the latest homologation provisions (but for only one season), which allowed them to swop cylinder heads: a 1.3ltr version of the BDA engine was developed. Vince Woodman and Gillian Fortescue-Thomas drove what were effectively works-backed 'RS1300s'.

These 190bhp cars were invincible in their capacity class where Woodman won five times and privateer Peter Hanson four times. This, though, was the end, as for 1974, the British Saloon Car Championship was run to Group 1 rules: cynics dubbed this 'Group 1½' as there was more freedom than in the strictly-applied International category. This meant that the RS1600 and the 190bhp 'RS1300' were henceforth banned in the UK.

16-VALVE ESCORTS IN THE EUROPEAN TOURING CAR CHAMPIONSHIP

With the Twin-Cam no longer competitive in Group 2 European races, Ford held back until 1971, when the more promising RS1600s appeared instead. There were too many retirements for this to be the Escorts' year, their efforts being overshadowed by the 'works' Capris.

With a 1.8ltr TJ-injected engine, the German-built Fitzpatrick/Mass car finished fourth overall at Monza after a puncture, then won the 2ltr race at the Salzburgring. Problems then set in – a broken prop shaft at Brno, differential failure at the Nurburgring (when leading overall), a broken flywheel at Spa, and a time-consuming shunt at Paul Ricard. Consolation came at the end of the season, at Jarama, Spain, where Fitzpatrick and Jochen Mass won outright.

1972 was more promising. This time using a Boreham-backed 1.8ltr car with a 260bhp Hart-BDA, Gerry Birrell/Claude Bourgoignie won the 2ltr class at Monza, and there were similar great performances for other cars during the year, including fourth for Dave Matthews/Andy Rouse in the

The Greek Acropolis rally was always rough, tough, dusty and hot. Bjorn Waldegard won the 1977 event in this RS1800.

By winning the 1977 RAC rally in this British Airways-sponsored car, Bjorn Waldegard notched up the Escort's sixth consecutive RAC success.

When Ford workers went on strike in 1978, Ford contracted out their RAC rally effort. David Sutton's team built this RS1800, and Hannu Mikkola drove it to victory. No problem!

Broadspeed car at Circuit Paul Ricard, and third overall/class win for Tom Walkinshaw's David Wood-built car in the British TT.

For 1973, though, there was no factory interest – the massive budget went into the Capri RS2600s, while Ford-of-Britain spent all its funds on the latest rally cars.

Apart from the first appearances by beautifully-prepared Zakspeed cars (Heyer/Mohr won their class in the Zandvoort four-hour race), and a remarkable fourth place in the TT by the Spanish pair (Uriarte/Leguellac in a Broadspeed car) it was a very quiet season indeed.

Zakspeed

First you have to draw breath, and learn to spell the company's names – for it was Erich Zakowski who set up his tuning business, Zakspeed, in Niederzissen, close to Germany's Nurburgring.

Born in East Prussia (a satellite of pre-Hitler Germany), then moving to Schleswig Holstein, and finally opening a truck dealership at Niederzissen in 1960, Zakowski started racing in 1968 – using a self-prepared Escort 1300GT with a Broadspeed engine.

By 1973 Zakspeed was building and developing most of its own Escort parts, this being the year in which Dieter Glemser won the German Touring Car Championship. In 1974, with much help from Ford-Germany, Zakspeed effectively became the 'works Escort' team, its beautifully-presented RS1600s winning the European series (led by Hans Heyer): the very same car (driven by Dieter Glemser) also won the German series.

More success followed in Germany in the late 1970s, but before long Zakspeed moved up to Group 5 racing, and to developing a series of highly modified Capris. At the same time the company developed the special wheel-arch kit seen on so many other Mk II Escorts, along with a series of limited-production road cars for Ford-Germany.

Later still, in the mid-1980s, but with no conspicuous success, Zakspeed turned to F1 racing, and all links with Ford were lost.

If French vandals had not shovelled rocks in his path on a special stage, Bjorn Waldegard would have won the Monte in 1979. As it was, he had to settle for second place.

But not in 1974. Ford-of-Germany campaigned Capri RS3100s against the latest BMW 3.0CSLs – yet Zakspeed's team won the entire European Makes Championship, and won the Driver's series too!

In a six-race series, the Zakspeed Escorts (which were really surrogate 'works' cars), magnificently-prepared, and heavily sponsored by Castrol and Radio Luxembourg, won the 2ltr category on every occasion (Hans Heyer was the lead driver), and also won the Nurburgring Six-Hour race outright. Although this was great news for Ford, it was an embarrassment for the Capris, which had more than 420bhp, and were supposed to be unbeatable!

Aiming for reliability rather than razor-edge performance, the Zakspeed cars used iron-block 2ltr engines which pushed out 'only' 275bhp, the Championship-winning car also using 15in (380mm) wheels with 14in (355mm) wide rear rims! This, let me remind you, was still a Group 2 series, which says much for the homologation expertise at Boreham (John Griffiths, in fact) which was being deployed.

Zakspeed's performance was so consistent that they wrapped up the Makes category with an event to spare, this being an ideal way to bring the career of the Mk I car to a close. For the time being, the European Touring car series then went into steep decline for, in the aftermath of the Energy Crisis, both Ford and BMW closed down their racing divisions.

RS1800 RACING IN EUROPE – LITTLE ACTIVITY

After all that excitement 1975 was a complete anti-climax. New regulations (*see below*) were pending, so neither Ford nor Zakspeed showed much interest in an interim year.

Double triumph for Ford in 1979, when the company won the World Rally Championship for Makes, with Bjorn Waldegard becoming Champion driver.

Heyer/Finotto took second place at Monza four-hour race in an old-style RS1600, but in the Nurburgring six-hour both cars retired – one with oil feed problems to the engine, the other without any oil in its back axle.

Then came the big change. Because of the regulations newly applied to Group 2 race cars in 1976, the RS1800s had to run at 1.9ltr, and race cars were obliged to use wet-sump engines. Early on, Zakspeed's RS1800s suffered so many surge-related engine failures that they were withdrawn for the rest of the season.

When dry-sumping was once again allowed from mid-1977, Zakspeed returned,

Backed by Rothmans' millions and David Sutton's expertise, Ari Vatanen became World Rally Champion in 1981. VLE 756X was brand new for the RAC rally, finished second, and was never rallied again.

to prove a point. In the Nurburgring six-hour race Hans Heyer/Armin Hahne finished a remarkable third overall – behind a BMW 3.0CSL and a Jaguar XJ5.3C.

Zakspeed built new RS1800s for the 1978 season, entered four European rounds, and amazed everyone (especially the BMWs!) by once again winning the Nurburgring six-hour race outright, its drivers being Werner Schommers and Jorg Denzel.

Amazingly, the ageing RS1800 was still competitive in 1979. In a thirteen-round series (which included two British events) the two Zakspeed cars with Klaus Niedzweidz and Sigi Muller as lead drivers took three second places overall, three third places, and were fourth five times; they were totally dominant in the 2ltr class.

This, though, was close to the absolute end for rear-drive Escorts in motor racing, as the ETC had now lost every scrap of its remaining prestige. Ford would not be interested again in top-line motor racing until the arrival of the Sierra in the mid-1980s.

6 Hopes Dashed – Escort RS1700T

If the stillborn Escort RS1700T had been a lasting success, any number of people would have claimed credit for its birth. For a time everyone looked on it as the next of a distinguished series of 'works' Escorts. Yet in the end the project was cancelled, and there is now a long line of Ford people who insist that it was not their idea!

There's no doubt that *as a competition car* the RS1700T concept was a great idea in 1980, very promising in 1981, and still viable in 1982 – but after that it was killed off by events. If the Audi Quattro had not appeared, four-wheel-drive rally cars might not have evolved, and the RS1700T would probably have been the world's fastest rally car in the mid-1980s.

If the RS1700T had been backed enthusiastically by Ford's planners and financial

In 1979 Ford Motorsport built a 'Fiescort' prototype, in which an RS1800 engine and drive line was somehow shoe-horned into a Fiesta structure. Effectively, this was the forerunner of the Escort RS1700T.

number-crunchers, instead of being merely tolerated as a cuckoo in the corporate nest, all might have been well. The problem, though, was in finding powerful personalities to back it, and in finding somewhere to build the production run.

If Ford Motorsport had been managed, at the time, by more influential personalities, all might still have been well. Unhappily, director Mike Kranefuss was promoted to a Ford-USA position before the very first car was built, while his successor Karl Ludvigsen was new and relatively unknown at Ford.

ANALYSIS

The seeds of the RS1700T story were sewn in the late 1970s, when the Escort Mk II was still the most famous rally car in Britain. Ford Motorsport realized that this legendary machine could not go on for ever, and set out to replace it. More power, better traction – in fact more of the same – seemed to be the way to go.

The impetus came in 1979, when Ford decided to put Boreham's activities into hibernation after it won the World Championship. No sooner had Ford Motorsport won the World Rally Championship for Makes (and Bjorn Waldegard the Drivers' Crown) at the end of that year, than Boreham started looking to its future.

There were many outside influences, such as what the competition might do and

Mike Kranefuss

The man who started as a Ford Motorsport departmental manager in Germany became Ford's worldwide motorsport boss in the 1980s, then moved out to run his own teams in the USA. Mike Kranefuss also presided over the famous 'works Escorts' motorsport team at Boreham in the late 1970s.

Originally helping to run the first Ford-Germany rally Taunus cars, and then working on the Capri RS2600 race cars, Mike became competitions manager in 1972. When Stuart Turner moved out of Motorsport in 1975, Mike then became Director, Motorsport, Ford-of-Europe; apart from regular liaison meetings he left Peter Ashcroft to run Ford-UK's motorsport efforts.

Mike was in charge from 1975 to 1980, a period when the 'works' Escorts gradually became supreme at World Rally Championship level. It was Mike who imposed the closedown of Boreham's rallying activities at the end of 1979, and who encouraged investigations that led to the RS1700T project.

Mike, too, aided the start of the Escort RS1600i programme, but he was then promoted yet again – this time to Detroit, to revive Ford-USA's motorsport programme, and soon to take responsibility for the mainly USA-financed F1 programme. It was at Mike's insistence that Cosworth was invited to produce the turbocharged 1.5ltr V6 F1 engine of 1985, and the new-generation HB F1 V8 which followed in 1989.

In 1993, though, he walked away from Ford-USA, after a total of twenty-five years' service with Ford, to set up his own motor racing business – Penske-Kranefuss Racing of North Carolina – where he was in partnership with Roger Penske, running a stock-car team.

new regulations that were brewing, and the conundrum of where to have production cars manufactured.

World motorsport authorities were already discussing a new regime of rallying at this time, which would include Group N, Group A and Group B categories, and although four-wheel drive had finally been authorized from 1 January 1979, only Audi seemed to be taking that provision seriously.

Having talked things through with his boss, Mike Kranefuss, and his drivers, Peter Ashcroft concluded that the 'works' team needed a new rear-wheel-drive Group B car, of which only 200 so-called 'road' cars would have to be made to achieve homologation.

Boreham's brief was to look at Ford's present and future model range, to decide on which model family looked the most promising, and to evolve the layout of a new model. There was no way, it was thought, that a totally unique car could be designed – it would have to be a modified version of an existing Ford.

But, until the 1990s, how much did we really know about the background story of the Escort RS1700T's troubled life? That it was the early-1980s rear-drive Escort that matured while four-wheel-drive rally cars

Under the design leadership of ex-Porsche engineer John Wheeler (third from left, back row), Boreham designed and built the first front-engine/rear-drive Escort RS1700T in 1981. Karl Ludvigsen, Ford's Vice-President of Governmental Affairs and Motorsport, is centre rear in this group shot.

were already on the scene? And that it was broadly based on the structure of Ford's first front-wheel-drive Escort? But what else?

Did you know, for instance, that RS1700T test cars were quicker than the Lancia Rally 037s which went on to become World Championship winners in 1983? And that there might have been a four-wheel-drive RS1700T as well – and that Boreham's celebrated engineer, John Wheeler, had already sketched that up by mid-1982? And that certain elements of the RS1700T 4×4 layout were carried over to the Escort RS Cosworth of the 1990s?

I learned a lot from a straight-from-the-horse's-mouth interview which designer John Wheeler gave me, many years after the still-born RS1700T was laid to rest.

John had not originally started his career by designing competition cars, for he studied mechanical engineering at Dundee University then fell in love with motor cars, and motor car engineering, and secured a job at Porsche in Germany.

He started on Porsche production lines, including assembling engines and transmissions, then from 1972, eventually working in the engineering department, in the 'advanced design' department. From 1974 he settled in the chassis design/development area. This

was where the RS1700T connection was really forged, for at this time he was working on original concepts for the Porsche 928 – which just happened to have a front engine, rear transmission, and a robust torque tube connecting them. Does that sound familiar?

Then, in 1980, he saw an advert in *Autosport* which was seeking a designer for a new project: 'Having been over to the Silverstone Six-Hour race,' John recalls, 'I then visited Peter Ashcroft, talked about the new job – and the rest you know.'

By mid-year John had been hired to work at Boreham, actually arriving in October 1980, just as design work on a new car was about to begin:

> There was the intent to do a new car, and the previous rally engineer, Allan Wilkinson [along with Len Bailey], had already had a 230bhp BDA-engined/rear-drive Fiesta built, with a Mk II Escort front end and a longitudinal engine mounting, a front-mounted clutch, and a large diameter propshaft running back to a Hewland FGB five-speed transaxle.

This was very much of a 'look-see' car that had independent rear suspension, which king mechanic Mick Jones instantly

Although it was based on the new-generation transverse-engine/front-drive Escort, the RS1700T had a longitudinally-positioned engine driving the rear wheels.

christened a 'Fiescort', and which Boreham coded P1.

> From my Porsche experience – both the 924 and the 928 had front engines and rear transmissions – as soon as I saw it, I knew that it was a technical non-starter – that large-diameter prop shaft, with all its inertia, would not still be running smooth at 9,000rpm!
>
> Even so, it was a great little test car, which we all enjoyed driving, but I had a new brief. A new front-wheel-drive Escort, the Mk III, was coming on the scene, and all the marketing interest was to do a car on that base, for it was this Escort they wanted to promote. In any case, we all thought the Fiesta was a bit small, too short, with limited wheel travel.
>
> At that time the first Audi Quattros were in existence, and known, but not yet rallying. We still thought there was considerable doubt as to whether four-wheel-drive was the way to go.

To clarify the performance of all types, and to compare rear drive with front-wheel drive, in 1980 Ford not only kept Hannu Mikkola's 1979 RAC-rally-winning Escort RS, but also built a 230bhp BDA-engined front-wheel-drive Fiesta. Back-to-back testing at several Welsh special-stage venues, with Stig Blomqvist driving, were conclusive – that the front-wheel-drive installation was over-powered for the package.

It took at least another decade until the world's rally engineers learned how to tame the high output of a front-wheel-drive rally car: even by the year 2000 all such cars still struggled to find traction on loose-surfaced special stages, and the Fiesta-BDA fared no better. John remembers:

> Pretty soon, the team was convinced that rear-wheel-drive was the way to go, and I think we were all convinced that we could develop a very competitive package. We were looking at using 300–350bhp, so we chose to use a turbocharged engine. At this time, incidentally, we also did four-wheel-drive studies ...

It was also at about this time that Karl Ludvigsen, Ford's Vice-President in charge of motorsport (Peter Ashcroft's new boss, who had taken over from Mike Kranefuss when Mike was promoted to run Motorsport in the USA) also decided that the team should take a look at the one-off Ghia-styled AC3000ME sports car, which was mid-engined and used a Ford 'Essex' 3ltr engine.

John and his small team (there were only four designers at Boreham at this time), however, studied the mid-engined layout, did not like the high-speed handling implications, particularly where the need to change the car's attitude on loose-surfaced stages was concerned, or those of accessibility for rally service 'in the gutter', and recommended that it should be rejected.

Detail design of an Escort-based car coded 'Columbia' then went ahead with great urgency (officially from 24 November 1980, though Wheeler's team had been beavering away for weeks before that date!), and was well under way by the end of the year. The first car to be finished carried the 'P4' identity, and was the first non-running RS1700T to be shown in public in mid-1981.

('Columbia', incidentally, was a name lifted from the USA's space shuttle programme, which was evolving with great success at the time. This was the name given to the very first shuttle to complete its mission in April 1981.)

Although the layout of the entire Ford 'Columbia' project was inspired by Wheeler, he still does not call himself the only designer:

> I used to scheme things out, and spend hours laying out the transmission and suspension installations, but I didn't draw it all up, not by any means.

The RS1700T used a Mk III body shell (as used in the later RS1600i and RS Turbo models – *see* subsequent chapters), but with very significant front-end structural changes, the addition of a big prop-shaft tunnel, and with a complete extra sub-frame added to the rear to support the transaxle and the multi-link independent rear suspension. 'It was a very significant carve-up,' John recalls, 'which meant that it was never going to be easy to build the production run ...'

Boreham's John Griffiths was closely involved in turbocharging the BDA engine, reducing its size to 1.78ltr so that (according to the FIA's regulations) it could still go rallying as a '3ltr' at reduced weight limits, and calling it the BDT. Incidentally, to provide a quick comparison at the testing

This was the layout of the original RS1700T, as captured by Terry Collins's 'X-ray' drawing of the period. Note that the gearbox is in the rear, in unison with the final-drive assembly.

Fitting a turbocharged BDT engine into the RS1700T bay, which was originally intended for transverse engine mounting, was surprisingly straightforward. Road cars would have had 200bhp, rally cars about 350bhp!

stage, and as a yardstick against the BDT, one of the early cars was fitted with an F2-based and very powerful Hart 420R engine – a non-Ford engine, this example actually being a normally-aspirated 2.4ltr four-cylinder with about 300bhp: 'But once we got the BDT running, we realized just how much more torque it had ...'

That car was P7, and was the machine later destroyed in Ari Vatanen's high-speed accident on a Portugal testing session.

The intention was that the homologation run of road cars should have been sold with a restricted-boost 200bhp engine and with a synchromesh gearbox, while the first 'works' rally cars could have used 350bhp with a 'dog' gearbox.

Other features included provision for almost everything to be a 'quick change' component (essential for rally servicing), this including a quick-shift five-speed gearbox (non-synchromesh 'dog' box for 'works' cars, synchromesh for road cars), and independent rear suspension and large wheels:

We provided huge wheel travel, which was good for traction. At the rear we also had

fully-adjustable linkages – anti-squat, anti-dive, and toe-in control – so that we could get the ideal set-up. We found that very minor changes could make a big difference to the traction – a 5mm (0.2in) difference in the ride height could transform the car, it was that critical ...

Compared with the rear-drive Fiestas, a project which Wheeler really inherited when he arrived at Boreham, 'Columbia' had one major innovation – the use of a light but massive aluminium torque tube which linked the engine solidly to the rear-mounted transaxle. This was a complete re-design of the racing-type Hewland FGB, and was packaged upside down to improve the weight distribution. This gave lightning-fast gearchanges, and seemed to be totally reliable.

FGB? In typically agricultural Hewland language, FGB was an acronym for 'F*****g Good Box'; it had been designed by Hewland himself, and by Mike Endean, for single-seater race car purposes.

According to John, whose technical reasoning can soon leave a mere motoring historian way behind, the torque tube was critical to the entire project: 'There were

Not a line out of place – and what a pity the RS1700T was outdated by the new generation of four-wheel-drive cars! This was the very first RS1700T prototype to be completed.

already several examples of how to run a rear transaxle in a car – very good examples from Porsche, and poor examples from Alfa Romeo ...'

Positioning the heavy clutch/flywheel assembly, keeping the prop-shaft in balance at high speeds, and packaging everything under the floorpan all had their effect. So, drawing on years of Porsche experience, John replicated what 'Porsche always did', using three intermediate prop-shaft bearings around a long quill shaft which linked front to rear: 'The inertia of an open two-piece prop-shaft would have been too high, and it would soon have knocked out the synchromesh on road cars.'

When the RS1700T project went public at the Nurburgring in mid-1981, there was only one definitive prototype, and John had already realized that the time-scale was almost bound to stretch:

> With all such projects, there is rally car design, and then there is production car design, which are two totally different things. We could always create the rally cars within Boreham's four walls, and we could have been rallying in 1982, but the production cars, well ...

Rod Mansfield's team at Ford's SVE department was then persuaded to take up the development and 'productionization' of the road cars – and almost immediately uncovered all the problems and legislative hang-ups. From this point it was always intended that the 200-off run (fewer numbers were sometimes quoted – for Ford could have included all the prototypes in its 'minimum run' figure) was to take place at Saarlouis, but work was still not complete when the project was finally cancelled in March 1983.

In the meantime, the projected capital cost of tooling, and of carrying out the major carve-up of front-wheel-drive body shells into those suitable for rear-drive mechanicals, had rocketed from an initial £170,000 to more than £271,000.

> Although we got a lot of support from Karl Ludvigsen, and Saarlouis were very helpful (the Pilot Plant were involved in making up low-cost press tooling for the special panels), this was always going to be a difficult project, to build 200 cars through the Ford production system.

Almost immediately, it seems, the cars proved to be very rapid in testing, and had tremendous potential, and John was soon convinced that Ford Motorsport had a competitive tarmac test car: 'But at that stage the Audi Quattro had already started winning events, and setting different standards.'

Like all dedicated engineers, John liked to experience what he had designed, so as rally-car testing progressed he spent more and more time in the co-driver's seat:

> I was pretty scared to start with, but it got better – I was more scared, incidentally, in later years, when we started testing the RS200 in Portugal! That was a combination of speed, heat, and the sheer commotion of what was going on.

From mid-1981 Pentti Airikkala, Markku Alen, Malcolm Wilson, Hannu Mikkola and Ari Vatanen all tested the cars, in Wales and in Portugal, using actual rally stages where times achieved by other rally cars were already known.

Particularly in Portugal, where cars were tested on stages recently used in a World Championship rally, the RS1700T was phenomenally fast, even in less than perfect conditions – though John's memory of the way that Ari Vatanen crashed one of the cars (P7, the Hart-engined car), and the way that car and crew had to be rescued from a ravine, many feet below the level of the mountain road, is the sort of story that enlivens one-make club dinners for years!

Even in May 1982, incidentally, there was a weight reduction problem to be addressed; although the '3ltr' class limit was only 1,958lb/940kg, the test cars tended to weigh in at around 2,400lb/1,088kg, which was the equivalent of carrying two extra passengers at all times.

By mid-1982 a four-wheel-drive version was being proposed, with John Wheeler producing a closely reasoned analysis of what could be achieved, and what *should* be achieved on the RS1700T base.

The RS1700T retained much of the new Escort XR3's structure, including the rear hatchback, but had its own unique rear spoiler, bumper and wheelarch extensions.

This paper, fascinating to historians, suggested that the two-wheel-drive RS1700T would still be a potential winner on tarmac, but would be uncompetitive (against the Quattro) on gravel and snow by the end of 1983 and: 'The success of the Audi Quattro has proved that even a relatively bad four-wheel-drive configuration can be made to work acceptably ...'.

There was no doubt in John's mind that the Quattro was a very crude answer to the four-wheel-drive installation problem! John thought that the production run of rear-drive RS1700Ts should be built, but that the prototype of a four-wheel-drive version, much-modified in almost every way (with the gearbox up front, next to the engine, perhaps), could be running by mid-1983, and enter rallying by the beginning of 1984: 'The four-wheel-drive option is an essential back-up for a large company involved seriously in motorsports ...'.

Yet nothing came of this – in higher management, Karl Ludvigsen was still short of influence, and at some levels there almost seemed to be a Ford mind-set against four-wheel drive – which doomed the RS1700T to a short life at top level.

Of the rear-drive car, though, Wheeler insists that:

> The reality was that what we had developed was right for seven-eighths of Ford's competition world, but wrong for the final eighth, which was the 'works' team competing at the top level. That was the dilemma.

By 1983, rear-drive RS1700T prototypes were already formidably fast rally cars, and were still competitive with the Quattro. Testing carried out in mid-Wales showed them to be between three and five seconds a mile quicker than the best of the Mk II Escorts and the rear-drive Opel Mantas – between fifteen to twenty seconds on a five-mile stage, which was a phenomenal improvement.

Even in rear-drive form, by the way, Wheeler was already studying an 'evolution' version, a lighter and more powerful car with much improved weight distribution, more weight moved backwards, better tyres and much suspension development. Although the original car lacked power-assisted steering, John reckons that it would have been needed as development, and tyre widths, increased.

The problem, though, was that the production-standard road car was not yet ready, and even though cars approaching the road-car specification of trim and equipment had been built by the end of 1982, there was still work to be done. Complete with all the equipment (including Recaro seats, electric window lifts, stereo, and all the other gear essential for marketing purposes) this could have been a 2,500lb/1,134kg road car. Both Boreham and SVE were struggling to get this version released, and cars produced in numbers.

CANCELLATION

As we all know, the RS1700T was abruptly cancelled within days of Stuart Turner taking over from Karl Ludvigsen in March 1983, this being one of the first of several decisive actions Turner took at the time of his re-appointment. As Stuart had already written in an earlier briefing for Walter Hayes:

> We must accept that the new Audi will be a *formidable* competitor, and that in 2WD form the RS1700T will struggle to beat it ...

And this:

> Any car which, like the RS1700T, takes an eternity to come to life, makes me nervous ...

115

But, later on in his autobiography, he commented that:

> I was genuinely sad that the RS1700T had to go. For more than two years Boreham had sweated on the development of this car, often without much help from other areas of Ford ...

At first, apparently, Ford had hoped to sell such cars for £23,000 each (which, in 1981, compared very badly with the £5,692 asked for an XR3!), but this price also rocketed as the months dragged on. No definitive price was ever fixed, and the evidence of the sales performance of the RS2000 that followed suggests that sales would not have come easily.

Except that the engines and transaxles were saved for future use, all the investment in this new model had to be written off. I have no doubt that previously-published estimates of at least £4 million are reasonable. By Ford standards, maybe that was peanuts, but it was still serious wasted money.

As soon as Turner had recommended cancellation to the Product Strategy Group on 14 March 1983 ('... the discussion before the axe fell took less than five minutes ...'), he called Peter Ashcroft, and work stopped that day.

The press release which followed noted Turner's opinion, that:

> Having spent some time looking hard at our existing plans, I have become convinced that we are not moving in the best direction if we are going to resume our former position in international motorsport.

And that was that. Boreham stopped working on the cars, for rally use, for road car

By the end of 1982, Boreham had a workshop full of RS1700T prototypes, some for rally testing, and some for development as road cars.

Karl's official title was Vice-President, Motorsport and Governmental Affairs, one of his important briefs being to develop a fresh motorsport strategy, which had to follow Boreham's withdrawal from World Championship rallies.

Unhappily, no thought was being given to the clubman at first. Boreham's new project, the complex Group B Escort RS1700T, was being designed, and the brutal Cosworth-powered C100 Group C racing sports-car was on the way – but nothing was being developed to succeed the fast-selling Mk II RS models, particularly not the RS2000.

Ford Motorsport of Germany were convinced that they needed a new Escort-based model (for motor racing, rather than rallying), because they wanted to promote its use in the new-fangled Group A category.

This meant that at least 5,000 cars were needed to gain sporting homologation – and of course Motorsport wanted this to be very rapidly indeed. When approval came, Lothar Pinske's engineers in Ford-of-Germany Motorsport began modifying the new XR3 (the fuel-injected XR3i was not even being considered at this stage), to idealize it for their purpose.

This was no simple tune-up and dress-up job – when the RS1600i eventually went on sale, Ford issued a 'Unique Parts List' which totalled fourteen closely packed typescript pages!

IMPROVING ON THE XR3

In many ways, the latest Escort was a much more promising car on which to complete a transformation than the rear-drive cars had ever been. The all-new platform featured a transversely-mounted engine, a brand-new transmission and front-wheel-drive, while there was independent suspension at front *and* rear.

Ford Motorsport, Germany

From a standing start in January 1968, Ford-Germany's motorsport department began winning events within a year. They won the European Touring Car Championship in the early 1970s, and later were only hit by brutal budget cut-backs.

Jochen Neerpasch was the first manager of a Cologne-based operation, Mike Kranefuss was his deputy, and Martin Braungart was an important engineering contributor. First with Capris, later with Taunus 20Ms in rallying (they won the Safari in 1969, a miraculous result), and then with Escorts at all levels, Ford-Cologne soon became a formidably successful team.

Britain's Walter Hayes controlled the finances, and although Stuart Turner had nominal control from 1970 he tended to leave well alone. After their own Capris had tasted success, the team backed Zakspeed, but from 1975–76 the department was no longer directly involved with Escorts.

Ford advertised this machine as 'Simple is Efficient', and the only imponderable was its new type of engine – the single-overhead-cam CVH (Compound Valve-angle Hemispherical chamber) which was being built at a new factory at Bridgend, in South Wales. To be made in 1100, 1300 and 1600 forms, it came complete with an aluminium cylinder head, a cogged belt to the overhead camshaft, hydraulic tappets, and was meant to be an eventual replacement for the gently ageing Kent push-rod power unit.

Drivers rapidly found that the hydraulic lifters 'pumped up' soon after the rev counter needle passed 6,000rpm, and there was always a suspicion that this unit might not be as free-revving as the legendary Kent. Ford made no apologies for any of this, as this was an engine meant to look after the exhaust emissions regulations of the 1980s and 1990s. Motorsport, to them, did not enter into their calculations.

It is important to stress the XR3, rather than the XR3i, connection. Even though the RS1600i sold alongside the XR3i for more than a year, it was previewed in Germany at least a year before the XR3i was introduced. Accordingly, it kept the same basic three-door XR3 hatchback body structure, Weber-carburetted engine, transmission and suspension layouts, though wherever possible these were improved to make them more suitable for motor racing.

The RS1600i was the very first Escort to use a five-speed version of the modern transversely-mounted front-wheel-drive transmission, which had originally been introduced with an all-synchromesh, all-indirect, four-speeder. To meet the latest trends, a five-speed derivative (effectively with an 'overdrive' fifth ratio) was speedily evolved, the RS1600i being the first user, months ahead of any other Escort.

Because of time and financial constraints, the German engineering team's options were therefore strictly limited. For the engine, not only did Bosch K-Jetronic fuel injection replace the dual-choke Weber carburettor, but there was a new camshaft profile, a modified cylinder head and porting, different exhaust manifolding and solid (instead of hydraulic) valve lifters. It was the last change, in particular, which raised the hopes of engine tuners.

This was the very first application of Bosch fuel injection to Ford's new CVH engine (the XR3i version, which used the same basic hardware followed on later, with totally different plenum chamber and throttle body detailing), the whole package being designed to meet the latest exhaust emission regulations.

Here was an engine that felt altogether more sporting than that of the XR3 – yet it

Similar, but not identical, to the Escort XR3i engine which followed, the RS1600i's power unit was the first CVH type to use fuel injection. The message on the camshaft cover was crystal clear.

was little more powerful, and no more responsive, than the XR3i which really evolved from it.

These peak power figures, all made freely available in 1981 and 1982, tell their own story:

XR3	96bhp (DIN) at 6,000rpm
RS1600i	115bhp (DIN) at 6,000rpm
XR3i	105bhp (DIN) at 6,000rpm

The RS1600i engine could easily have delivered more, but apparently it was German insurance problems which limited the RS1600i's power output: with solid valve lifters it could certainly have been made to perform better than this. As we soon realized in 1982, tuned versions for use in Group A motorsport could produce at least 150bhp at 7,000rpm. In the UK, Richard Longman's 'Datapost' race cars proved this on the circuits in 1983 and 1984.

Because of budgetary limitations, there was little scope for major suspension and

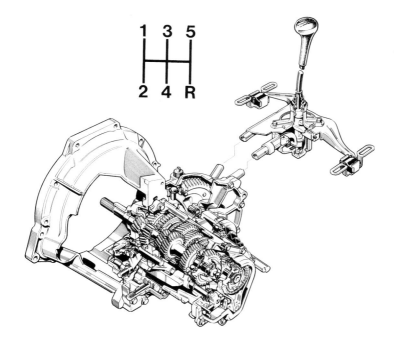

Ford's five-speed gearbox for front-wheel-drive cars went into production at the start of 1982, the RS1600i being the first model on which it was standard. In improved form this, the 'B5' layout, was still in use at the start of the 2000s.

chassis improvements. Although the existing suspension layout was not changed, spring and damper rates were all altered. At the front there were separate anti-roll bar and adjustable drag links to locate the decambered front struts more accurately than before. The front suspension was adjustable for castor – and although this was not the sort of detail you or I might fiddle with for road use, it was considered to be of vital interest to race track preparers.

At the same time 15in diameter seven-spoke alloy wheels with 6in (152mm) rims, and fat 50-section tyres, were chosen (these were the lowest profile tyres yet to have been offered on a Ford road car), while the front ride height was cut down, and harder-rate Koni dampers were chosen.

There were very few changes to the body shell itself, though any number of minor identification points were detailed in information put out by the factory to their dealers when the car was current.

Surprisingly, the XR3's 7in (178mm) rear brake drums were retained (bigger rears would already have been available, and the XR3i would in any case get bigger brakes, but nothing was done). Owners reckon that these have never been a problem on their cars, as 'most of the effort is at the front anyway ...'.

All in all, the RS1600i had a mean, get-out-of-my-way stance, with enough rubber on the road, and the right kind of wheels, to impress bystanders. XR3is, up to a point, could be driven by anybody (and were often not appreciated), but every RS1600i seemed to go to a customer who knew *why* he was paying a premium price. This certainly wasn't a mass-production Escort – allied to its performance, and its behaviour, there were enough visual clues to prove that point.

There are two important detail points which should be made:

• The very first Ford-UK brochures (dated October 1982) mentioned a rear anti-roll bar in the specification, though the wording of these brochures was then changed in January 1983 – such bars do not seem ever to have been fitted.

• Even on the standard-production road cars, the Koni dampers were adjustable for stiffness rating, though not for ride height. However, for this to be done,they had to be stripped, compressed,then adjusted by carefully following a set of service instructions. My guess is that very few such tasks were ever tackled, but now you know.

Visually, the RS1600i was made distinctive with new paint jobs and new types of front and rear spoiler, while there was a unique striping package, better front seats, and (for the UK market) a four-spoke RS steering wheel, along with a useful but drag-enhancing set of four extra auxiliary lamps.

The result was that the RS1600i felt (and looked!) harder, twitchier and altogether more 'race-track' than the XR3, and was usually described by testers as a more nervous, throttle-sensitive machine. If the XR3i had not arrived so soon afterwards, the RS1600i would probably have been described as the best-handling front-drive Escort of all. It was a low, hard-sprung hot hatch, and the car was very 'chuckable'.

In a test of an early UK-market car (this being published in February 1983), *Autocar* described the handling as 'distinctly twitchy', and commented that:

> The RS1600i is a more nervous, throttle-sensitive car below the limit than the XR3i ... There are two main areas of complaint – straight-line stability and braking ... despite the low-profile tyres and increased roll stiffness, the RS1600i has a very good primary ride. The ride, it could be said, is very good and entirely in keeping with the nature of the car.

The first turbocharged CVH engine was developed at Boreham in 1981, on the basis of the carburetted XR3 power unit. The turbocharger itself was mounted neatly behind the front grille (to the right of this picture), with an intercooler positioned alongside it.

The new model was first revealed in September 1981, in left-hand-drive form, at the Frankfurt Motor Show, but deliveries did not build up properly until 1982. In the meantime, Bill Meade got the job of re-engineering the car for right-hand-drive production (most of the work was concentrated in the engine bay), the result being the UK-market car's launch at the Birmingham (NEC) Motor Show in October 1982.

British enthusiasts loved the car, especially in its revised form from May 1983, when the XR3i chassis changes (including a new front cross-member and revised suspension geometry) were adopted. RS fanatics didn't mind that the RS1600i was no faster than an XR3i, and they didn't mind the expense either – it was special, it *looked* special, and it *handled* in a special way, too.

PRODUCTION AND UK SALES

Although Ford-Germany originally set out to make exactly 5,000 RS1600is, so that it could qualify for Group A motorsport, there was so much demand that the run had to be extended. A total of 8,659 RS1600is were manufactured between 1982 and 1984: 2,608 were sold in the UK.

The vast majority were UK-registered in 1983. The last few cars, incidentally, seemed to take ages to move out of the showrooms, as these official UK registrations prove:

Year	RS1600is sold in the UK
1982	47
1983	2,545
1984	10
1985	4
1986	2
Total	*2,608*

Ford-Motorsport's Escort Turbo Championship, new for 1983, provided valuable experience for the future. The carburetted turbo kits helped produce 125–130bhp.

In 1984, after a short life, the RS1600i was displaced by the first-generation Escort RS Turbo, which shared some of its chassis technology, but had more power, much more potential, and also boasted a viscous-coupling limited-slip differential in its transmission.

For a time the RS Turbo took the limelight, and RS1600i values collapsed, but within five years an RS1600i 'classic' cult had grown, there was a big demand for surviving cars, and values began to rise again.

Then came the recession, and the Great Insurance Scam, which hit the RS1600i's value, if not its image, very hard indeed. Even so, many owners love their cars so much that they put up with any financial insult to keep them on the road.

The queue starts over here...

Escort RS1600i (1982–1984)

Layout

Unit construction steel body/chassis structure. Two-door plus hatchback, front engine/front-wheel drive, sold as four-seater sports hatchback.

Engine

Type	Ford CVH
Block material	Cast iron
Head material	Cast aluminium
Cylinders	4 in-line
Cooling	Water
Bore and stroke	80.0 × 79.5mm
Capacity	1,596cc
Main bearings	5
Valves	2 per cylinder, directly operated by single overhead camshaft, bucket-type tappets, and rockers, with the camshaft driven by cogged belt from the crankshaft
Compression ratio	9.9:1
Fuel supply	Bosch K-Jetronic fuel injection
Max power	115bhp @ 6,000rpm
Max torque	109lb ft at 5,250rpm

Transmission

Five-speed manual gearbox, all-synchromesh

Clutch	Single plate, diaphragm spring

Overall gearbox ratios

Top	3.187
4th	3.648
3rd	4.877
2nd	7.334
1st	12.096
Reverse	13.901
Final drive	3.84:1

(20.6mph (33.2km/h)/1,000rpm in top gear)

Suspension and steering

Front	Independent, by coil springs, MacPherson struts, track control arms, radius arms and anti-roll bar
Rear	Independent, by coil springs, transverse links, radius arms and telescopic dampers
Steering	Rack-and-pinion
Tyres	195/50HR-15in radial-ply
Wheels	Cast alloy disc, bolt-on fixing
Rim width	6.0in

Brakes

Type	Disc brakes at front, drums at rear, hydraulically operated
Size	9.4in front discs, 7.1 × 1.25in rear drums

Dimensions (in/mm)

Track	
Front	54.5/1,384
Rear	56.3/1,430
Wheelbase	94.5/2,400
Overall length	159.5/4,051
Overall width	62.5/1,588
Overall height	52.6/1,336
Unladen weight	2,027lb/919kg

UK retail price

At launch in 1982	£6,700

'White Lightning', the original Escort RS Turbo road car, went on sale at the end of 1984. Having evolved from the original Motorsport turbo kit, the road car engine featured fuel injection, and there was an FFD viscous coupling type of limited-slip differential, along with flared wheel arches and an Orion-style grille to match.

Escort RS Turbo (1984–1986)

Layout
Unit construction steel body/chassis structure. Two-door plus hatchback, front engine/front-wheel drive, sold as four-seater sports hatchback.

Engine
Type	Ford CVH
Block material	Cast iron
Head material	Cast aluminium
Cylinders	4 in-line
Cooling	Water
Bore and stroke	80.0×79.5mm
Capacity	1,596cc
Main bearings	5
Valves	2 per cylinder, directly operated by single overhead camshaft, bucket-type hydraulic tappets, and rockers, with the camshaft driven by cogged belt from the crankshaft
Compression ratio	8.2:1 (Nominal)
Fuel supply	Bosch KE-Jetronic fuel injection, plus Garrett AiResearch T3 turbocharger
Max power	132bhp @ 6,000rpm
Max torque	133lb ft at 4,000rpm

Transmission
Five-speed manual gearbox, all-synchromesh
Clutch	Single plate, diaphragm spring

Overall gearbox ratios
Top	3.245
4th	4.056
3rd	5.423
2nd	8.156
1st	13.450
Reverse	15.457
Final drive	4.27:1

(20.3mph (32.7km/h)/1,000rpm in top gear)

Suspension and steering
Front	Independent, by coil springs, MacPherson struts, track control arms, radius arms and anti-roll bar
Rear	Independent, by coil springs, transverse links, radius arms, anti-roll bar and telescopic dampers
Steering	Rack-and-pinion
Tyres	195/50VR-15in radial-ply
Wheels	Cast alloy disc, bolt-on fixing
Rim width	6.0in

Brakes

Type	Disc brakes at front, drums at rear, hydraulically operated
Size	9.4in front discs, 8.0 × 1.5in rear drums

Dimensions (in/mm)

Track	
Front	54.5/1,384
Rear	56.3/1,430
Wheelbase	94.5/2,400
Overall length	159.8/4,059
Overall width	62.5/1,588
Overall height	52.6/1,336
Unladen weight	2,150lb/977kg

UK retail price

At launch in 1984	£9,250

No Escort enthusiast could ever ignore the original RS Turbo of 1984–86, which not only had RS1600i-type wheels and fat tyres, but flared arches, and the sort of badging which caught everyone's attention.

Escort RS Turbo S2 (1986–1990)

Layout
Unit construction steel body/chassis structure. Two-door plus hatchback, front engine/front-wheel drive, sold as four-seater sports hatchback.

Engine

Type	Ford CVH
Block material	Cast iron
Head material	Cast aluminium
Cylinders	4 in-line
Cooling	Water
Bore and stroke	80.0 × 79.5mm
Capacity	1,596cc
Main bearings	5
Valves	2 per cylinder, directly operated by single overhead camshaft, bucket-type hydraulic tappets, and rockers, with the camshaft driven by cogged belt from the crankshaft
Compression ratio	8.2:1 (Nominal)
Fuel supply	Bosch KE-Jetronic fuel injection, plus Garrett AiResearch T3 turbocharger
Max power	132bhp @ 6,000rpm
Max torque	133lb ft at 4,000rpm

Transmission
Five-speed manual gearbox, all-synchromesh

Clutch	Single plate, diaphragm spring

Overall gearbox ratios

Top	2.903
4th	3.629
3rd	4.851
2nd	7.296
1st	12.033
Reverse	13.828
Final drive	3.82:1

(22.6mph (36.4km/h)/1,000rpm in top gear)

Suspension and steering

Front	Independent, by coil springs, MacPherson struts, track control arms, and anti-roll bar
Rear	Independent, by coil springs, transverse links, radius arms, anti-roll bar and telescopic dampers
Steering	Rack-and-pinion, with power assistance
Tyres	195/50VR-15in radial-ply
Wheels	Cast alloy disc, bolt-on fixing
Rim width	6.0in

Brakes	
Type	Disc brakes at front, drums at rear, hydraulically operated, with mechanical ABS
Size	10.2in front discs, 9.0 × 1.75in rear drums

Dimensions (in/mm)	
Track	
Front	54.5/1,384
Rear	56.3/1,430
Wheelbase	94.5/2,400
Overall length	159.3/4,046
Overall width	62.5/1,588
Overall height	52.6/1,336
Unladen weight	2,247lb/1,017kg

UK retail price	
At launch in 1984	£10,028
'Custom' pack cost	£572

BLOWING IN THE WIND

When the Escort RS Turbo appeared in 1984, it startled Ford's Escort buyers. With a turbocharger and a limited-slip differential, it pushed Escort technology to new heights. If you had mentioned this sort of thing back in 1968, people would have laughed at you.

Startling? For sure, and once again I'm writing here from real experience – long-term experience. I kept an Escort RS Turbo in the family for more than four years, and around 40,000 miles (64,360km). The first time I set eyes on an Escort RS Turbo it looked impressive enough, but that was before I had even driven it. The first time I floored the throttle through a roundabout, a silly grin flitted across my face. Here, for the first time, was an Escort that felt fast enough *and* could put its power down to the road.

Previously, my XR3i had been brisk, and quite nimble, but there was always the chance of getting wheelspin and understeer, and the thought that you would eventually run out of steam. With the RS Turbo, there was more grip away from the traffic lights, and especially on tight corners. No-one who sampled an RS Turbo ever raved about other people's GTIs again.

Yet, do you remember how impressed we used to be by Mk II RS2000s which could beat 110mph (177km/h)? Do you also remember thinking that the end of the sporting world had come when the last rear-drive Escorts were built? So you must also remember what a nice surprise the arrival of the Escort RS Turbo was.

Go on, admit it. When the RS1600i went on sale, we all thought we could see the trends – and we were all wrong. By 1983 the Mk II RS2000 had been dead for three years, and there seemed to be nothing more exciting in the pipeline.

Then came the rebirth. And what a rebirth – not only was this a new RS-badged Ford that offered real innovation, but it was the first series-production turbo Ford, and the world's first road car to use a viscous

Because of the noticeable turbo lag in the engine, there was a right and a wrong way to make rapid progress in an Escort RS Turbo. How do I know? Because I owned one for a couple of years in the 1980s. Until the Escort RS Cosworth came along, this was the fastest of all Escorts.

coupling limited-slip differential as standard.

To use horse-racing terms, the original RS Turbo was by SVE and Boreham, out of RS1600i, but many had an input. One way or another Stuart Turner, Rod Mansfield, Bill Meade, John Griffiths, Karl Ludvigsen and Lothar Pinske were all involved.

As developed by Special Vehicle Engineering, the car which went on sale in 1984, the all-white 132bhp 'homologation special', was very different, in detail, from the first prototypes. First there were two different turbocharging kits, then a project to build a rally

car, next a proposal to build a mere 5,000 machines, and finally an Escort flagship which was built for six whole years. Welcome to the ever-changing world of Ford product policy.

Although the RS Turbo project was born in April 1983 and put on sale before the end of 1984, a need for such a car had been identified well before that. Three of Motorsport's experienced engineers, Bill Meade, John Griffiths and Terry Bradley, had designed and developed a turbocharged XR3 prototype in 1981, this one using forced-induction to a dual-choke Weber carburettor.

The final RS Turbo styling package of 1986–90 included a more rounded nose, bonnet louvres, new-style wheels, extra plastic sills under the doors, and a re-shaped rear spoiler. Under the skin, though, the 132bhp turbocharged CVH engine was much as before.

special, and made available in a full range of colours, the revised car sold strongly for another four years.

Introduced in mid-1986, the definitive RS Turbo was just as powerful as before, though there was more sophisticated control of the ignition and engine fuel supply. In so many ways, this was now a softer and more sophisticated machine.

Special Vehicle Engineering's enthusiasts re-worked the chassis without losing the character, making it subtly and successfully more of a road car than a de-tuned competition car. There were new features in the suspension (which lost its RS1600i-type linkage), the transmission and the brakes, and a new look (including a new style of cast aluminium wheel) to make the changes obvious.

To make this a more relaxed road car, the overall gearing was raised (the final drive ratio had been changed from 4.27:1 to 3.82:1): when using 4,000rpm in fifth gear the latest car cruised at 90mph (145km/h), whereas the old car would have been doing a mere 81mph (130km/h). For high-mileage users like me, that was the good news. For the traffic-light cowboys, though, the bad news was that the new car didn't accelerate quite as rapidly as before. Even so, it was still good enough to see off most of the imported competition.

But one had to understand the engine, and the shape of the torque curve. If you pottered around town in fifth gear, then floored the pedal at the 30 limit, it took time to light up and get going. The first time my wife drove the car, and did this, she was most disappointed. My reaction was merely to blurt out: 'Wait!', and after a few seconds all was well. Lots of torque soon came rushing over the horizon, and the VC took care of the rest.

Yet if you changed down every time the RPM needle dropped below 3,000rpm, the turbocharger was always spinning rapidly, and response was immediate. The RS Turbo, in fact, was really two cars in one – there was the hard-and-fast turbo hatchback, but there was also the smooth, I-don't-want-to-make-a-fuss-about-anything, suburban cruiser.

Then there was the suspension, changed amid some controversy for the 1986 model. Mine felt fine, for the traction and poise was still there, in full measure, but compared with the original type this was a softer version. The braking was even better than before, because there were larger front and rear brakes, plus the option (for about £300) of the new-fangled Lucas-Girling Stop Control System, a mechanically-sensed type of anti-lock facility, not nearly as advanced as the usual Teves or Bosch ABS layout. On my car, this rarely kicked into operation, but when it did I could certainly feel the mechanism pulsing back through the brake pedal.

Style changes included new sill extensions linking the front and rear wheel arch bulges, a new nose (common to all other Escorts), cooling louvres in the bonnet panel, and a different (less effective, surely?) type of rear spoiler. Cars fitted with the Custom Pack (most were) had electric window lifts, a sun-roof and central locking. All cars, naturally, were fitted with Recaro front seats, the best in the business.

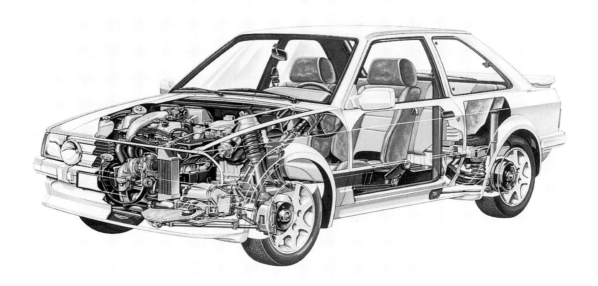

The Escort RS Turbo of 1984 was neatly packaged, with a bonnetful of turbo power, and with those exclusive seven-spoke alloys for recognition.

The RS1600i's fascia/instrument panel, though all new, was clearly related to the earlier types that had gone before.

Even though RS Turbo prices started at £10,028 (Custom Pack an extra £572) in mid-1986, customers continued to flock, drooling, to Uncle Henry's showrooms; the records show that more than four times as many were sold, compared with the original 'White Lightning' type.

By 1988 the turbocharger had a water-cooled centre bearing, the engine an anti-knock sensor, the Custom Pack had become standard – as this also included a high-spec radio/stereo cassette, tinted glass, rear seat belts and full instrumentation, Recaro seats (need I go on?) – it is easy to see why RS Turbo prices crept up to £13,985 by mid-summer 1990.

The end of the Escort RS Turbo, however, was not the end for the CVH-Turbo engine, which found a home, modified in many ways, in the short-lived Fiesta RS Turbo. In that car the turbocharger was smaller and the electronics more advanced, but the effect was just the same – paralysing performance and great character.

ESCORT RS TURBO – THE IMPORTANT DATES

October 1984: Launch of original Escort RS Turbo production model.

December 1984: Series production of

Escort RS Turbos began.

June 1985: Homologation into Group A (5,000 cars completed by this date).

December 1985: Last original-style RS Turbo built. Total production 8,604, of which 5,576 were sold in the UK.

Then a half-year gap until:

July 1986: Introduction of facelifted RS Turbo 'S2', using the 'Mk IV' Escort nose style, with bonnet louvres, modified wheel arch extensions, and sill extensions.

1987–88: 'Basic' specification progressively withdrawn. Only 'Custom' versions available by mid-1988.

Summer 1990: Last Escort RS Turbo built.

Ford Escort performance

Mark III and Mark IV, front-wheel-drive models

This is a summary of the figures achieved by Britain's most authoritative magazine, *Autocar*, of cars supplied for test by Ford over the years:

Model	Escort RS1600i Mk III 1,596cc 115bhp	Escort RS Turbo Mk III 1,596cc 132bhp	Escort RS Turbo Mk IV 1,596cc 132bhp
Max speed (mph)	116	125	124
Accn (sec):			
0–60mph	8.7	8.1	9.2
0–80mph	15.0	13.1	14.1
0–100mph	27.9	21.2	23.0
Standing ¼–mile (sec)	16.9	16.2	16.8
Consumption (mpg):			
Overall	28.3	26.8	27.4
Typical	33	30	30
Kerb weight (lb/kg)	2,027/919	2,150/975	2,247/1,017
Year tested	1983	1985	1986

8 Front-Wheel-Drive Racers – in Motorsport

In the 1980s Boreham was populated by enthusiasts – even if its controllers did not always agree with what was proposed. Accordingly, when the Escort RS1600i eventually came along as a road car in 1982 and 1983, Ford-Germany Motorsport *and* Boreham saw it as ideal for a Touring Car Championship 'class car' racing.

Peter Ashcroft invited Dorset-based Richard Longman to run a pair of cars for him in the BTCC. The surprise was that Richard accepted so readily, for he had suffered one very frustrating season in Fords –

in 1980, when he had tried, and failed, to make the Fiesta competitive.

But that was then, and this was later. For 1983 he was ready for a further challenge. For the 1,600cc 'baby-car' category, the Escorts looked as if they might produce up to 160bhp and more, and might even be dominant in their class.

Once he had analysed the possibilities, Richard make the project successful – triumphantly, and very rapidly indeed. Ford provided the cars, Datapost (the Royal Mail's high-speed delivery service) and

The highspot of the RS1600i's 'works' rally career came in November 1983, when Malcolm Wilson won his class in the RAC rally.

Kyosti Hamalainen, who had once won the 1,000 Lakes rally in an RS1800, drove this Escort RS Turbo in the 1,000 Lakes of 1985.

Duckhams a great deal of sponsorship, and Avon furnished the rubber, while Longman himself found the power. Richard told me:

> Our development actually started by working with Rod Mansfield's SVE department to improve the handling. The rear suspension wasn't very good at first, and we had to change the pick-up points to cut out a lot of the rear-end steer.
>
> The original 1983 cars needed to improve, even at the end of the year, so for 1984 we changed the shells, incorporated those changes, and they were a lot better after that. The handling was so good by then that, for the very first RS Turbo race car of 1985, I just converted one of the RS1600is instead of building a new car.
>
> We did all our own engine development – camshafts, pistons, breathing, the lot – we didn't have engines from anybody else. We found that the CVH was very prone to detonation – but we sorted that, and ended up selling engines to other teams in Europe.

Longman Engineering was perfectly capable of tackling such a ground-up job, for Richard Longman (once a mechanic at the famous Downton Engineering business)

had gathered together an amazing amount of expertise.

In the first season though, quite amazingly, it was a private Escort RS1600i driven by Chris Hodgetts (his car being prepared by Brooklyn Ford of Redditch) which provided most of the competition to the Datapost team, and by the end of the year his machine was competitive with the works-backed examples.

As *Autosport*'s seasonal survey for 1983 commented:

> All three Escort men were hampered at the beginning of the season by a lack of preparation time and homologated bits but [by the end] ... managed to take six wins to a total of only four from both VW Golf and Scirocco.

In an eleven-round series, the Escort glory was shared – with Hodgetts winning three times and the Datapost cars three times (Alan Curnow twice, Longman himself only once). It was only by finishing every race that a VW Golf GTi driven by Alan Minshaw beat them to a Championship class win.

Longman, a ferocious competitor for whom the phrase 'good loser' was unknown, decided that he needed to do much better in

1984 – and did. As already noted, he re-shelled both his cars, carried out a lot of handling development, and faced the new season with much more confidence.

This time he easily outpaced Chris Hodgetts – seventy-four points to forty-five was a colossal margin – by winning his class in six of the eleven events (Hodgetts won only twice), but the RS1600i monopoly of the 1.6ltr category was even more impressive than that. Longman's team-mate Alan Curnow also won once and was usually well-placed immediately behind the battling duo: no other make of car got a look-in.

By consistently scoring so many points, Longman came close to winning the Championship outright – he finished second overall, and would undoubtedly have won if he had not got involved in another car's accident at Brands Hatch on 'British Grand Prix' day, and also at Thruxton.

By any standards 'Car 77' (Richard ran with the same competition number all season) set a series of remarkable performances, and was still not at its peak. If he had not been determined to shoot for outright victories in future (and Ford had not tempted him to do just that with the new Escort RS Turbos), he might have blotted out any further competition in future years.

Even though the Datapost effort was to be split in 1985, the RS1600i success story had further to go. Eight different cars scored Championship points in 1985: Chris Hodgett's car won the category – and also finished second overall to series victor Andy Rouse's Merkur XR4Ti. Hodgetts won six classes, Richard Belcher four times, and Alan Curnow's Datapost car just once.

For Ford, this sort of consistency also helped them to win the Manufacturers' prize – which made all the efforts worthwhile. One of the 1984 Datapost RS1600is was eventually converted to become the

Richard Longman

Both as a racing driver, car tuner and builder, Richard Longman brought real flair to the Datapost Escorts in the 1980s.

As a mechanic with Downton, then with Janspeed, Richard learned more than anyone else about the tuning of BMC A-Series (and, later, other companies) engines, and became an acknowledged preparation expert. He also raced.

After founding Richard Longman Engineering in the early 1970s, he was then involved in a bad single-seater racing accident. Once recovered, though, he prepared Mini 1275GTs and won the British Saloon Car Championship twice in succession – in 1978 and 1979.

The Ford connection followed almost at once, when he ran 1.6ltr Fiestas in the 1980 BTCC. Returning to British Leyland, he then ran Metros for two years, but was tempted back to run the famous Datapost Escorts from 1983 to 1986.

At first with RS1600is but, from 1985, with the 270bhp Escort RS Turbos, he tamed the Escort's front-wheel-drive chassis so well that his rivals sometimes wondered how he was getting round the regulations. But he wasn't cheating – just extremely resourceful and diligent.

Datapost withdrew their sponsorship at the end of 1986, and as the phenomenally powerful Sierra RS500 Cosworths were also coming on stream in 1987, Richard saw that there was no way of winning races outright with the Escort RS Turbo, so closed down the project.

Richard continued to develop his business, producing the 'works' Peugeot engines for the BTCC, and other customers continued to keep the Christchurch operation very busy.

first of the RS Turbos, Alan Curnow's car was sold off in the UK, and the spare car ended up racing in the Far East.

FORCED-INDUCTION RACERS

Richard Longman's legendary Datapost Escort RS Turbo might only have been used for two seasons in the BTCC – 1985 and 1986 – but they were phenomenally successful. Richard's team only ever needed to build three cars – one for himself, one for his second driver Alan Curnow, and one as a spare: the spare was rarely needed.

From June 1985 to the end of 1986, the Datapost cars were the fastest Escorts so far built – and it showed. Ford, as usual, gave Richard Longman the ultimate challenge – they provided hardware and money, Datapost, Avon and (this time) Esso chipped in with the balance, Richard provided the tuning expertise and the racecraft, and results were expected.

They arrived, spectacularly and often. By doubling the power of the engines – road cars had 132bhp, the Datapost cars raced with 270bhp ('and sometimes we'd qualify with 300bhp') – sorting out the handling, and praying that the turbochargers would stay in one piece, the Datapost RS Turbos were *always* potential class winners.

Even against Andy Rouse's turbocharged Merkur XR4Tis, Rover SD1s and big BMWs, Richard's RS Turbo usually finished in the top six overall, occasionally even getting a podium finish. Always quicker in the opening laps, when tyres and the turbocharger were in 100 per cent condition, with more turbocharger reliability it would have been invincible. Even so, it was always competitive, and often promised to be an outright winner.

But these were not discreet little race cars. Class wins are one thing, but giant-killing acts are another. Sitting there, on the grid, engine off, the bright red Escort looked impressive enough, but firing it up brought a new dimension.

There was no silencer, of course, and a massive exhaust drain pipe poked out under the driver's door, the paintwork around it completely burnt away. At idle – lumpy, noisy and bubbly – that big exhaust pipe sounded merely hoarse, and rather tentative. Revved up, pre-green flag, that bubble became a drone. Then, once moving, the drone became a full-throated, gruff roar. Gear change points? About 7,500rpm. Red

Louise Aitken made her name in the Fiesta Ladies' Championship, but soon progressed to more senior rallying. She drove this RED-prepared RS1600i on the Swedish rally of 1984.

line? 8,000rpm. When did you last get those sort of figures out of an RS Turbo road car?

RS TURBO – TAMING THE BEAST

Richard's work on turbocharged Escorts started early, well before a race programme was suggested, with track tests of the carburettor-turbo CVH engine:

> We put that engine, modified, with a different radiator, different suspension and stuff, into one of the RS1600i race cars, and tested it at Donington Park. That went quite well ...

To gain Group A homologation, 5,000 road cars had to be built – and counted – but because the RS Turbo didn't get into production until the end of 1984, that wasn't finally achieved until 1 June 1985:

> Because of this, we were six months behind the others [in the 1985 BTCC]. We had to sit out the first few races, so we carried on

driving the RS1600is. But it wasn't all bad news. We got rid of a lot of the problems before we were allowed to race. Even so, we didn't have to make excuses after we'd been testing all the previous winter – because we hadn't ...

From day one, the bright red RS Turbo's pace was explosive, even when (because of the turbocharger 'multiplication' formula which effectively made the engine capacity much higher) obliged to run in the 1.6–2.5ltr class. With only one such race car in 1985, the new projectile was amazingly fast. On Silverstone's GP circuit it was only three seconds a lap slower than Andy Rouse's 300bhp Championship-dominating turbocharged Merkur XR4Ti, and that gap would be narrowed in the following season.

With an official 250bhp immediately available (but up to 270bhp most of the time), Richard had only one immediate problem, as this *Autosport* report confirms:

> Richard Longman campaigned the Ford Escort RS Turbo ... which exhibited truly breathtaking straight line speed, if a dislike

Before its programme started in 1985, Boreham's 'works' Escort RS Turbo looked extremely purposeful. With substantial sponsorship from British Telecom radiopaging, Mark Lovell had an extremely well-supported programme.

Ford launched the 1985 'works' Escort RS Turbo rally programme from a barge on the Thames, upstream of London's Tower bridge. The 200bhp car, complete with a battery of six Lucas driving lamps, looked better than it was to perform. Mark Lovell (left) and co-driver Peter Davis, though, were not to blame.

for slowing down, and turning corners. When the car is fully developed, it is going to be very hard to beat ...

Which it was, in short order, with newly-homologated big brakes, with even wider wheel rims, and a lot of tyre technical help from Avon. By the end of the first season, this wasn't just a slingshot little monster with a crude chassis, but a carefully-engineered and extremely effective chassis.

Boreham changed a lot on the rally cars, but we kept the aluminium front cross-member, basically keeping the RS1600i race car front end, but a different RS Turbo race car rear end.

FIERCE UNDER THE SKIN

This bright red BTCC Escort was pure stripped-out racer, able to run to the minimum weight limit, and to carry ballast to trim the handling. The roll cage was nicely integrated, the instrument panel bristled with ECUs and auxiliary controls, while the sills were laced with mysterious fluid pipes.

Dominated by its intercooler, and acres of aluminium-shaded lagging to keep the temperatures down, the engine bay was full – so full that an engine oil cooler had to live under the rear floor, behind the rear suspension, which explains the braided pipework threading its way through the cabin.

9 ACE – the Escort RS Cosworth

Peter Ashcroft, Mike Moreton, John Wheeler, John Griffiths and Bill Meade and I used to get together at Boreham regularly for meetings about the future.

I think we were all agreed that whatever our next rally car would be, it had to be based on the platform and the basic layout of an existing mainstream model ... This time we wanted to plan well ahead, for the 1990s, and we wanted to start at once.

I think it was one of my comments, thrown into the conversation, that encouraged a breakthrough: 'Why don't we see if we can take the platform and running gear from a Sierra Cosworth 4×4, shorten it, then see if an Escort body will fit on it?'

So says Stuart Turner. Romantic? Yes. Fictional? No, this really was how the Escort RS Cosworth was conceived. The elements of a new front-wheel-drive hatchback shell were somehow made to fit the shortened platform of an entirely different four-wheel-drive saloon. It all happened in 1988, though the production car would not go on sale for another four years.

I suppose I should have known that something important was brewing at Boreham at this time, when Mike Moreton used to tidy up his office and cover a flip chart before I was even allowed in through the door, and when engineer John Wheeler began floating around with that familiar Cheshire Cat 'I'm working on something big and secret' smile on his face. I'd already

seen that expression before – once when the Escort RS1700T was being designed, and once when the famous RS200 was on the way.

But there was a protocol to be observed. At Boreham, when great schemes were coming together, you didn't ask questions. At best you'd get a rude answer, and at worst you might find that you were not even allowed in through the gate next time around.

So I waited, and waited. Rallies came and went. The three-door Sierra Cosworth matured, won the Tour de Corse, and gave Jimmy McRae another British Rally Championship victory. Prototypes of the Sierra Cosworth 4×4 breezed in and out of the workshops.

The unmistakeable silhouette of the Escort RS Cosworth was finalized with hundreds of hours of wind-tunnel testing. The high rear spoiler was essential to promoting high-speed stability and positive downforce, the extracts behind the front wheels perfect for venting the front brakes.

Compared with ordinary front-wheel-drive Escorts, the Escort RS Cosworth had a different front end, with a large under-bumper spoiler, extra driving lamps, and vents in the bonnet panel.

Until one day I spotted a rather odd-looking Escort RS Turbo with people fussing around it. But *was* it an RS Turbo or not? Somehow, it stood more four-square than normal, with a wider track, with bigger wheelarch flares ... and there was something else. Yes! The wheels, subtly, were not in their normal positions – the wheelbase was longer than usual. The tumblers finally dropped into place when I heard the engine being fired up, and witnessed the unmistakeable drone of a Sierra Cosworth engine.

This was, in fact, the original 'mule' for the car we now know as the Escort RS Cosworth, which combined a shortened Sierra 4×4 platform with an Escort RS Turbo body shell –

the Turner/Wheeler/Moreton way of making a smaller and more nimble car than the Sierra Cosworth 4×4.

But why build such a car, with an obsolete style? Simply because it is easier to convince management about a concept they can drive than one which they can only study on paper. I think it was Ford's Bob Howe who once told me that: 'One running car is worth a hundred meetings ...'.

John Wheeler

London-born John Wheeler was always interested in automobile engineering, and came to Ford almost by chance in 1980, after spending years with Porsche. He was a rising star in the chassis area at Porsche (this including work on racing sports cars) when in 1980 he answered an *Autosport* advert – for a job at Boreham.

Once there, he led the team that designed the still-born Escort RS1700T, and lobbied in vain for a four-wheel-drive version to be developed. Later his concept for the RS200 evolved into the 200-off supercar, after which he became chief engineer on the rally-improvement of Sierra RS Cosworth cars. From 1988 he ran the new ACE (Escort RS Cosworth) project.

A spell as Aston Martin's chief engineer then led to his return to Ford's technical HQ at Dunton, where he began the 2000s working on a variety of secret projects.

CONCEPT

This 'Escort-Sierra' was the result of a mountain of analysis. By the late 1980s John Wheeler knew that all World Championship-winning rally cars needed four-wheel drive. There were many precedents.

By 1988, the Lancia Delta Integrale was dominant in World Championship rallying,

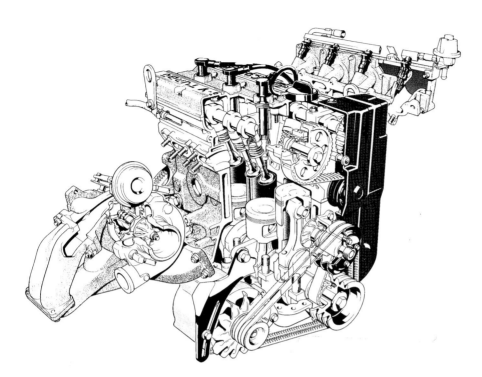

At the heart of the Escort RS Cosworth was a development of Cosworth's now-legendary YB turbocharged engine. Originally designed for the Sierra RS Cosworth (this drawing), it was further refined for Escort RS Cosworth use.

and Ford didn't enjoy that. They didn't like it at all. In a way, the 'works' team was still feeling cheated, for no sooner had the RS200 turned into a winning car (and, make no mistake, it was all set to start winning World Championship events in 1986) than Group B cars were banned. Was it no more than coincidence that Group A was imposed, and that Lancia just happened to have an ideal machine for that Group?

In the beginning, Wheeler and Moreton sat down to talk. Their object, quite simply, was to make Ford the world's most successful rally team. To do this, they needed to inspire the birth of a new car for Group A motorsport. At the end of the working day, they found time for a series of legendary, feet-on-the-table, sketching sessions.

Designing a competitive car was going to be demanding, but forcing it through Ford's management labyrinths was going to be very difficult. More than anyone at Motorsport, Mike Moreton knew how to do that. A veteran of AVO and SVE planning, he knew that it would have to survive committee meetings, presentations, driving demonstrations, and good, old-fashioned lobbying.

Wheeler considered every possibility. There were obvious constraints – 5,000 identical four-seater cars would have to be built to gain homologation, and the new car would have to be based on a lot of existing Ford hardware. To win in motorsport more than 300bhp was needed, it needed four-wheel drive, and it had to be as suitable for the Safari as the RAC rally, for Corsica as well as the Monte.

Any new Ford, therefore, needed to be better, a lot better, than the Integrale – and capable of improvement in the years which followed. And in basic form it had to be a practical road car – Ford would not approve the production of 5,000 identical cars if these could not be sold, and not make a profit.

Wheeler's analysis, later used as the basis of the presentation to the press, was masterly. Rejecting the new-type Fiesta as a basis, because it was physically too small to accommodate the engine, transmission and wheels that would be needed, and the forthcoming Mondeo because it was too large, and still too far into Ford's future, he settled on the cabin 'package' of the next Escort, the CE14 family.

Right from the start, too, he was determined to have a car that was aerodynamically stable – and if this meant that features even more extreme than those of the Sierra RS Cosworth were needed, so be it. The vast rear spoiler which transpired – at roof-top rather than mid-hatch level – proves that his point was made.

Compared with the Lancia, CE14 was larger and longer, but no heavier. The fact that there was a lot more space in the engine bay was considered important, for Wheeler wanted to eliminate under-bonnet heat-soak problems, to cater for all high-speed service and rebuild needs – and to find space for a lot of wheel movement in the bigger wheelarches.

Although the Lancia and other current rally cars all used transverse-engine layouts, Wheeler rejected that idea completely. An in-line engine, with a gearbox behind it, offered more, not only in terms of accessibility, but it idealized the weight distribution.

For such a new car, which Wheeler and Moreton coded ACE 14 (Group A CE14), developed versions of the Sierra Cosworth 4×4's platform and proven running gear would be ideal. Was it coincidence, or was it the sort of divine fortune that gifted designers always need, that the Sierra running gear fitted so well, and allowed development time to be telescoped?

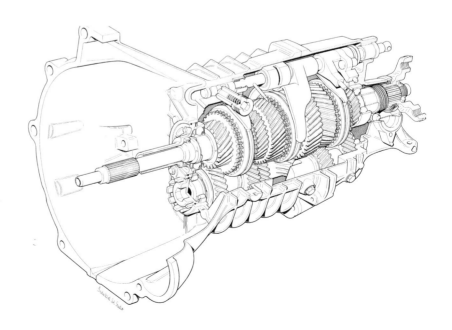

No problems with gearbox durability in the Escort RS Cosworth, for the MT75 unit which formed the base of the transmission had been designed to cope with cars as luxurious as the Scorpio, and as heavy and hard-working as the Transit van!

Escort RS Cosworth (1992–1996)

Layout
Unit construction steel body/chassis structure. Two-door plus hatchback, front engine/four-wheel drive, sold as four-seater sports hatchback.

Engine
Type	Ford-Cosworth YB series
Block material	Cast iron
Head material	Cast aluminium
Cylinders	4 in-line
Cooling	Water
Bore and stroke	90.82 × 76.95mm
Capacity	1,993cc
Main bearings	5
Valves	4 per cylinder, directly operated by twin overhead camshafts, via inverted bucket-type tappets, with the camshafts driven by cogged belt from the crankshaft
Compression ratio	8.0:1 (Nominal)
Fuel supply	Weber-Marelli fuel injection, with Garrett AiResearch TO3/TO4B turbocharger
Max power	227bhp @ 6,250rpm
Max torque	224lb ft at 3,500rpm

Transmission
Five-speed manual gearbox, all-synchromesh, and four-wheel-drive incorporating 34 per cent/66 per cent front/rear torque split

Clutch	Single plate, diaphragm spring

Overall gearbox ratios
Top	3.005
4th	3.62
3rd	4.923
2nd	7.530
1st	13.068
Reverse	11.801
Final drive	3.62:1

(22.28mph (35.9km/h)/1,000rpm in top gear)

Suspension and steering
Front	Independent, by coil springs, MacPherson struts, track control arms, and anti-roll bar
Rear	Independent, by coil springs, semi-trailing arms, trailing arms, anti-roll bar and telescopic dampers
Steering	Rack-and-pinion, with power assistance
Tyres	225/45ZR-16in radial-ply
Wheels	Cast alloy disc, bolt-on fixing
Rim width	8.0in

Escort RS Cosworth (1992–1996) *continued*

Brakes

Type	Disc brakes at front, discs at rear, hydraulically operated, with hydraulic ABS anti-lock control
Size	10.9in front discs, 10.8in rear discs

Dimensions (in/mm)

Track	
Front	57.2/1,453
Rear	58.0/1,472
Wheelbase	100.4/2,551
Overall length	165.8/4,211
Overall width	68.3/1,734
Overall height	56.1/1,425
Unladen weight	2,811lb/1,275kg

UK retail price

At launch in 1992:

Road Standard	£21,380
Road Luxury	£23,495

Development changes

From spring 1994, the specification was changed as follows:

Engine

Fuel supply	Ford EEC IV engine management system, with T25 turbocharger
Max power	224bhp @ 5,750rpm
Max torque	220lb ft @ 2,500rpm

Dimensions (in/mm)

Unladen weight	2,882lb/1,307kg

UK retail price

At launch in May 1994:

Road Standard	£22,535
Road Luxury	£25,825

DEVELOPMENT

Even though they really didn't have a budget, programme approval, or any spare time, Wheeler and Moreton then started a very expert scrounging process. Though the Sierra Cosworth 4×4 was still more than a year away from production, they acquired an engine and four-wheel-drive transmission from that car, along with a Sierra XR4×4 floorpan.

Working in secret, with expert help from TC Prototypes (who built up this car), the RS Turbo-based ACE 14 'mule' was built in a matter of weeks. Without anything formal such as drawings, John Thompson's team shortened the Sierra floor pan, inserted the RS Cosworth engine and transmission,

The YBT derivative of Cosworth's turbocharged engine was a neat fit into the bay of the Escort RS Cosworth. Complete with blue-painted camshaft covers, and a thoughtful shield over the top of the Garrett AiResearch turbocharger itself, it was a powerful (227bhp) and effective combination. Amazingly, my personal experience was that the battery never overheated.

grafted the modified Escort RS Turbo to it – and the original ACE was born.

This was the strangely-different 'Escort RS Turbo' which I had seen, which was eventually demonstrated to every decision-maker at Ford's Brentwood HQ, and which eventually convinced even the ditherers.

The rest is history. But doesn't it take a long time to turn a good idea into a production car? Although the Escort RS Cosworth rally car was officially previewed in September 1990, when Mia Bardolet won the Span-

ish Talavera rally on its world debut, and production cars went on sale in May 1992, it still took four years for the brainwave to be turned into the metal – and homologation was not achieved until 1 January 1993.

Every day, even so, was full of action, and negotiation. Once approved, the project was turned over to Special Vehicle Engineering for completion, Wheeler joining them as the chief project engineer. Along with Ford's stylists in the design department (and consultants MGA Developments of Coventry), SVE

Sexy, unique, and very functional, the Escort RS Cosworth fascia / instrument layout told a full story. The turbo boost gauge was in the auxiliary panel in the centre of the car. This was an early, pre-airbag-wheel, layout – and is, of course, a left-hand-drive car.

developed the hugely-effective aerodynamic package ('I knew we needed a rear wing as big as that,' Wheeler recalls, 'but I wasn't sure management would "buy" it at first.'), chose the 16in road wheels and produced a remarkably successful ride and handling package.

Along the way, they also oversaw the development of a more powerful version of the famous YB engine, and chose those unique instruments. The engine, by the way, might have been similar to that of the Sierra Cosworth 4×4, but had advanced in various ways, notably by using a hybrid TO3/T04B Garrett AiResearch turbocharger (it was really too big for road cars, but Motorsport needed it for full-house Group A tuning): cylinder heads were painted blue

instead of the Sierra Cosworth 4×4's green (and if you find one painted in red today, it may mean that it has been modified by one of the various tuning houses).

With 227bhp at 6,250rpm (and with a limited-duration overboost feature for overtaking), this Cosworth-described YBT engine was an extremely flexible power unit, naturally it ran on unleaded fuel, and an exhaust catalyst was standard.

There was much more to the styling changes – for the front and rear wings had to be reshaped, provision had to be made for exhausting hot air from the engine bay and the front brakes, a new high-tech instrument panel had to be laid out, and the entire package had to be made 'feasible' – possible, in other words, for manufacture in numbers.

Although this was always meant to be a supremely versatile road car – it had to pass all of Ford's ultra-demanding endurance tests (as an owner, I often had cause to bless this, for my own cars never overheated in heavy traffic jams, or failed to start on icy mornings), the Recaro seats not only looked welcoming but were superbly comfortable, while electric window lifts were engineered into the doors – it also looked as sexy as a Ford car ever could. Those five-spoke alloy wheels, 16in diameter with 8in (203mm) rims, looked so sensational that they were instantly copied by wheel makers all over the world.

Along the way, not only was this a car that developed positive aerodynamic downforce at all cruising and higher speeds, but it was 11.2in (285mm) shorter than the Sierra Cosworth 4×4. But no lighter, for a lot of work had gone into making this an extremely rigid hatchback: not that this mattered to the driver, for power-assisted steering and properly servo'd brakes were both standard.

During this period there was another huge stroke of luck for Ford, when FISA

Escort RS Cosworth

This is a summary of the figures achieved by Britain's most authoritative magazine, *Autocar*, of cars supplied for test by Ford over the years:

	Escort RS Cosworth T3/TO4B Turbo 1,993cc 227bhp	Escort RS Cosworth T25 Turbo 1,993cc 224bhp
Max speed (mph)	137	138
Accn (sec):		
0–60mph	6.2	6.3
0–80mph	10.7	10.9
0–100mph	17.4	17.9
Standing ¼-mile (sec)	14.9	15.0
Consumption (mpg):		
Overall	20.5	20.1
Typical	25	25
Kerb weight (lb/kg)	2,977/1,350	2,882/1,307
Year tested	1992	1994

announced a reduction in the production numbers needed to achieve Group A homologation, from 5,000 to a mere 2,500 cars. By pushing Karmann to concentrate on Escort RS Cosworth assembly at Osnabruck during 1992, Ford would easily have achieved its 5,000 target anyway in the first year (the limit, in fact, was on the number of engines which Cosworth could manufacture at Wellingborough), but having to build only half that number in the same time made the effort all the more comfortable.

The big breakthrough, in any case, had already come, when Karmann of Germany won the job of tooling the new structure, and manufacturing the production cars. In 1989, when the deal was done, Karmann was an ideal home for the new car – not only were they already producing the US-market XR4Ti (a modified Sierra), but they were also scheduled to build the new CE14-type Escort Cabriolet. No other company knew as much about the two principal elements of ACE, or was as resourceful in producing such special cars.

Preparations were completed using some of the old Merkur XR4Ti body framing and welding facilities (for that model most conveniently died before the Escort RS Cosworth was ready!), and once the team began assembling road cars early in 1992 the production rate built up rapidly.

PRODUCTION

In the first year, the rush was not only to build a lot of cars, but to make many of them suitable for use in motorsport. Although there was only one mechanical/chassis package, Ford's Product Planners then over-complicated matters by specifying three different trim/equipment levels throughout

Europe, starting with the 'Standard' (intended for motorsport) car, and topping out with the 'Luxury' version.

Incidentally, have you ever seen an Escort Cosworth without its huge rear spoiler? Perhaps not in the UK at all, but after the first 2,500 cars were built (to satisfy the homologation authorities about 'identical specifications') the car was certainly available in other European territories with the less extrovert option of only a single boot-lid spoiler. For motorsport use, however, the car was only homologated with the complete twin-spoiler equipment in place.

'Standard' cars lacked some of the gizmos most customers wanted (no tilt-and-slide sunshine roof, no electric window lifts, no radio-cassette equipment, no electrically-heated front window, and no fog lamps in the front apron), for Ford reasoned that these were items which would be cast out when motorsport preparation began.

Both cars, make no mistake, had excellent anti-theft precautions, including Ford's first-ever mainstream use of an engine immobilizer. The nation's low-life, however, took time to discover this – on one occasion

when my first car was parked outside a hotel overnight, they managed to butcher the door lock before discovering that the Vecta immobilizer had totally defeated them – I was happy about that!

In the UK, therefore, there were two prices – £21,380 for the 'Standard' and £23,495 for the 'Luxury' model (with an extra £481 charged for leather upholstery on the 'Luxury' version) – and a surprising number of lower-price 'stripped out' versions were actually delivered, which actually irritated Ford for a time as there was more profit for them in the better-equipped types.

The new car broke new ground – it was the first four-wheel-drive Escort and it was the first to have the name 'Cosworth' attached to it – and for a short time there was actually a waiting list, for Ford had pitched its prices very astutely. Well before the end of 1992, however, the rush was already over. In Britain the insurance industry had done its best to kill off the car's appeal, and theft or sheer bloody-minded vandalization had become a depressing feature.

Although Ford has never actually released detail figures, I understand that more than 3,000 cars were built before the end of 1992, that demand dropped back during 1993, and that by 1994 Karmann was not only building less than 1,500 cars a year, but that it was doing this by closing down the production lines for at least half of the working week.

Nevertheless, the new car got rave reviews wherever it was tested. Along with thousands of others, I was fortunate enough to own not one, but two (in succession) of the original spec cars in 1993 and 1994, both of them painted in that unique-to-Escort-RS-Cosworth colour known officially as Mallard Green (although SVE, I hear, always christened it as British Racing Duck!).

Following Boreham's sensational 1–2 finish in the 1993 Acropolis rally, Ford considered producing this limited-edition 'Acropolis' version of the Escort RS Cosworth – but did not go ahead with it. Note the air vents behind the front wheels, and under the rear bumper.

Trust the police to want to get their hands on the Escort RS Cosworth. Even when well-loaded up with extra gear, and a 'blues bar', this was still an extremely effective urban chase car. The Northumbria police bought several of these mean machines.

Problems? None at all – except that the 245/45ZR-16 Pirelli P Zero tyres wore out even quicker than I ever expected. So much so that I miscalculated the wear rate once, had a rear tyre literally explode on a motorway, and had to limp slowly home on the narrow-section, 'not over 50mph (80km/h)', space-saver spare tyre.

Even so, it was worth it, for the overall grip was matchless, and the ride was remarkable. As *Autocar & Motor* commented when comparing the new car with its deadly rival, the Lancia Delta Integrale:

> If you accept its fundamental firmness, the Ford's way with bumps is impressive. Edges are rounded, ruts and holes softened, and bumps smothered. No harshness, no jarring. Control and damping are simply brilliant.

Not that too many owners seemed content to leave the car as it basked in the showroom. As with the Escort RS1600 and RS1800 types before it, hundreds of standard Fords soon became competition cars – many for rallying, but a large number for

Cosworth Engineering

Founded in September 1958 by Keith Duckworth and Mike Costin, Cosworth was originally run on the basis that: 'It must be possible to make an interesting living, messing about with racing cars and engines.' Duckworth was always the design genius and Costin the development engineer.

The first Cosworth 'factory' was in the stable of the Railway Tavern in Friern Barnet, in north London, and the first Ford-based tuning project produced the 105E Formula Junior power unit.

Cosworth's first own-design cylinder head was on the SCA Formula 2 engine of 1964, its first twin-cam head being for the 1.6ltr FVA engine of 1967, and its first road-car engine being the original BDA of 1969 (for which Mike Hall did most of the actual design work).

By this time, of course, Duckworth had also conceived the legendary V8 DFV F1 engine, a power unit which sealed Cosworth's (and his own) reputation for all time.

Cosworth's BDA was their first road-car deal with Ford, this relationship becoming ever closer as the years passed, notably with the turbocharged YB (Sierra RS Cosworth/Escort RS Cosworth) and 24-valve Scorpio power units.

To follow the DFV, Cosworth also developed the turbocharged DFX engine for Indycar use, following with a series of new F1 and Indycar engines which brought major championships for Nigel Mansell (Indycars 1993) and Michael Schumacher (F1 1994). V10 F1 engines followed for Sauber, Stewart, Minardi and (from 2000) for Jaguar.

Cosworth lost its independence in 1980, then had several different parents before being split into two businesses in 1998. The motorsport section, Cosworth Racing, was acquired by Ford in September 1998.

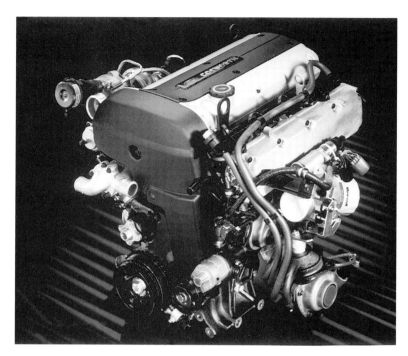

The later (1994–96) T25-turbo'd version of the Escort RS Cosworth engine is not at all well known, as it was not fashionable with the tuning shops. Compared with the 1992–94 variety, it had a different type of camshaft cover, the smaller turbocharger and many other new details.

racing and rallycross – which reduced the stock of road cars. Many owners, too, knew just what sort of reserves had been engineered in to this engine by Cosworth, and spent thousands of pounds in having the engines boosted to previously unimaginable heights.

We now know that true experts like Mountune could produce well over 350bhp, even while matching the engine to Group A regulations. Where the only limit was an owner's bank balance, it was possibly to add in various Sierra RS500 features (a large turbocharger, eight fuel injectors, and a bigger intercooler) and to liberate more than 500bhp.

No, I never actually drove such an Escort RS Cosworth but ... all I can say is that my two standard-specification cars, with 'only' 227bhp, were exciting road cars, so a fully-modified machine must have been mind-blowing.

MID-LIFE CHANGES

When my second car was delivered early in 1994, I noted that (like all other Fords of this period) the steering wheel had acquired an airbag, about which I was supremely indifferent, while the sunroof was now electrically operated. The performance, the ride and the general ambience, on the other hand, were still as superlative as ever.

Other changes, however, were on the way, these finally breaking cover in June 1994. Way back at launch time in 1992, Ford had already hinted that the original technical and visual package – big turbo, Weber-Marelli injection, whale-tail aerodynamics and a very basic 'Standard' specification – might be modified for 1993, then in the spring of 1993 it was suggested that changes would follow in mid-year; in the event none of these changes were made for another year.

With sporting homologation settled, the 'Mark II' Escort RS Cosworth finally appeared in preview cars in May 1994, being slightly less extrovert, even better developed than before, and yet more driveable.

This version of the car, which in the event would actually be rarer than the original, featured changes to the engine, to the general ambience of the interior and (optionally) to the styling.

The engine was the long-promised, and more flexible development, the YBP. Although, internally, there were few changes, and the maximum sustained boost was still limited to 0.8 bar, it now came complete with a smaller (T25) turbocharger which had 60 per cent less rotating inertia than before, corporate-style Ford EEC 1V electronics instead of the original Weber-Marelli, a revised throttle body, exhaust manifold, new HT coil arrangements and new-style/new-shape camshaft and drive covers.

The strategy had been to provide the same level of peak power (the quoted figure, in fact, was three bhp less but at 5,750rpm instead of the original 6,250rpm, while peak torque was developed at 2,500rpm instead of 3,500rpm) but with better driveability.

Those of us who had owned original-spec cars had been used to feeling the boost come in with a rush at about 3,000rpm, but here was an engine that pushed seamlessly from only 2,000rpm instead. Those who were used to changing gear at high revs would notice little difference, but those whose driving was a bit more relaxed immediately saw the point.

Not only that but, if you insisted, you were finally able to delete the big rear spoiler and its sturdy central pillar, though few real Escort RS Cosworth lovers in the UK ever seemed to do that.

Since 1992 Ford prices seemed to have see-sawed all over the place, but for the T25-turbo'd car there were still to be two versions, which were priced as follows:

Standard	£22,535
Luxury	£25,825

– added to which, leather seat trim cost £1,050, and air-conditioning £920.

Although the latest version was a fine car with a great sporting reputation – well over 5,000 original-type Escort RS Cosworths had already been built, and Ford Motorsport's fine record in World Championship rallies had made all the effort worthwhile – it arrived at an awkward time for the Blue Oval.

The Escort RS Cosworth's biggest problem was that because the entire Sierra range had been superseded by the Mondeo in 1993 (a car which was built on a totally different, transverse-engine, front-wheel-drive platform), it meant that the platform was no longer shared with any other Ford. The result was that because the Escort RS Cosworth was only being built in limited numbers that unit prices rose rapidly – and whenever Ford's all-powerful finance staff see those trends, they tend to reach for a plug to pull.

There was more. Car sales across Europe were still under pressure, the after-effects of an early-1990s trade recession, and the vicious (and, in my opinion, quite unjustified) attack on all such high-performance cars by the insurance companies all had an effect.

Not only that, but Ford had very definitely lost heart, lost faith even, in its 'RS' enterprise – and it wasn't long before rumours began to spread about the imminent demise of the Escort RS Cosworth.

For Ford-watchers, too, there was momentary confusion when the existence of two SVE-developed prototypes became clear, both of them based on the Escort RS Cosworth chassis, but with rear-wheel drive

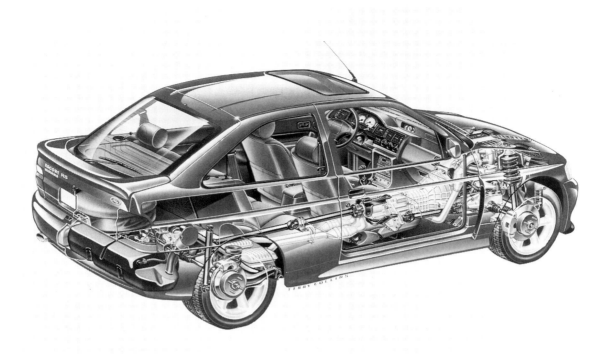

Even in this superb Terry Collins drawing, it isn't easy to see how the shortened platform of the Sierra Cosworth 4×4 was used as the basis of the Escort RS Cosworth. From 1992 to 1996, this was a fast and super-civilized road burner which could also be turned into a devastating rally machine.

– one with an RS2000 16-valve engine (*see* Chapter 11), the other with the torquey 2.9ltr twin-cam-per-bank Scorpio 24-valve power unit. Nothing became of either car, though both were seen in public after their development had been cancelled.

Well before the end of 1995, Ford had taken a decision – that the 'RS' era should be ended. The announcement came in September 1995, the Escort RS Cosworth was to be killed off in January 1996, and the excuse given was that the car could no longer meet the new exhaust emission laws, nor the latest 'drive-by' noise tests. (Production, in fact, could easily have been stopped in 1995, but by advertising a '1996' cut-off

date, this would allow Ford Motorsport to keep on using the car, and its planned derivative, the Escort WRC, for a further season at top level. Boreham's specialists, it seemed, had lost none of their guile.)

Some thought this a spurious excuse, while others accepted the inevitable. Richard Parry-Jones, Ford's vice-president of the small/medium vehicle technical centre, commented that: 'It's a sad day for hot-hatch fans. For a period at least, there will be no more high-performance Fords.'

But the dream was over. More than 8,300 cars had been built – and now there would be no more.

10 Escort RS Cosworth and RS2000 in Rallying – not Forgetting the Escort WRC

If we were honest, we'd admit that the Escort RS Cosworth was a rally car that went into production to gain homologation, not a road car that just happened to be a good rally car too. This was just one reason why the first rally car appeared nearly two years before road cars went on sale – and why it was an immediate winner.

When the new-generation Escort was approaching launch in September 1990, Stuart Turner realized that any pizzazz he could offer would help. There was a totally unexpected preview at Blenheim Palace, but this was only the start. Turner recalls:

> There was an ideal opportunity to run our first prototype rally car in September 1990, in the one-day Talavera Rally, in Spain, which had no homologation restrictions ...
>
> If we took the car out there, with one of our contracted teams – Mike Taylor Developments, with John Taylor running the team – and it failed, I reasoned that we could ignore the whole episode, and hope that no one had noticed. But if we succeeded, well, we could make as much noise as if we had won the Monte Carlo Rally.

The rest is history. Gordon Spooner Engineering built the car, Mia Bardolet drove it to victory, and, as Turner also quotes:

> Once the car had appeared in public, and a success ad had run saying 'First Time Out. First', I knew that it would be almost

First Time Out, First! An important victory for the prototype Escort RS Cosworth, driven by Mia Bardolet in the Talavera rally of Spain in 1990.

impossible for the company to cancel the project without huge loss of face.

For the next two years, development of rally cars went side by side with that of the 'works' Sierra Cosworth 4×4s, which shared much of their running gear. Far too much nonsense has been written, by others, denigrating the Sierras – but there is no doubt that they were almost extremely successful, especially in the 1992 World Championship season, and cruelly unlucky at times. That was the period, by the way, when the 'works' rally engines, complete with 40mm turbocharger restrictor, produced 340bhp at 7,000rpm.

Suspension breakage on the last special stage of the 1991 Monte cost Frenchman François Delecour outright victory, while in

In 1992, even before the car was homologated, Malcolm Wilson drove an Escort RS Cosworth to victory in the Hadrian Centurion rally. This was the car being fettled at a service point ...

1992 Delecour and the Italian Miki Biasion were on the World Championship podium four times, and Ford took third place in the Manufacturers' Championship.

Four-wheel-drive Sierras also won ten European Championship rallies, along with six National Championships in the same year – which should have been enough to silence the loud-mouths, but did not always succeed. This all provided a wealth of experience on which the 'works' team could draw.

During 1991 (and still well before the production car went on sale) Escort RS Cosworth development continued, with occasional rally appearances in Britain (where Malcolm Wilson's pace offered hope), and in Spain, where Mia Bardolet won several events in the Spanish Gravel series.

It was the same story in 1992. These cars used the very best of everything which had already been 'blooded' in the 'works' Sierra Cosworth 4×4s, including the 300bhp-plus YB engines (some said that the 'real' figure was 360bhp and more, but since the FIA was trying to limit power outputs, Ford

were saying nothing at the time), the *seven*-speed non-synchromesh gearboxes from FF, the larger front and rear axles (with 9in diameter crown wheel at the rear, and 8.5in diameter crown wheel at the rear).

Magnesium wheels, huge brake discs, massive brake callipers, Bilstein struts and dampers, different front crossmembers, different rear crossmembers, bag fuel tanks, and more, and more, and more, were all finalized. In the 1990s, more than ever before, well-specified Group A rally cars could be very special indeed.

In 1993 the only Escort RS Cosworth rally-car item still shared with the road cars was the body shell, and even then it was advisable for serious competitors to purchase a special assembly complete with welded-in multi-point roll cage and thin gauge skin panels.

And there was more. By this time the 'works' team and its associates had built up so much experience with the new car that they evolved two completely different 'packages' – one for its own 1993 'works' team, and another for the scores of private owners.

The difference between the chassis types was profound. For the private owners, who might want to create a new Escort RS Cosworth rally car by buying a new shell from Boreham, and then use almost all the running gear from their existing Sierra Cosworth 4×4 competition cars, new pieces were often interchangeable (or developed) from those of the 1990–1992 'works' Sierras.

In 1993, scores of 'new' Escort RS Cosworth race and rally cars were created like that – in fact Boreham's Motorsport Parts department started delivering bare, white-painted body shells before deliveries of road cars had even began.

For the 'works' team, though, John Wheeler and Philip Dunabin's test teams had established that there was a need for more suspension wheel movement to improve the traction, so for 'works' use only there was a new and integrated 'wide-track' package, with different springs, struts, dampers, track control and wishbone arms, anti-roll-bar kits, magnesium semi-trailing arms, drive shafts and steering gear. It wasn't possible to 'cherry pick' one or two items from this little lot – to make everything work it was either all or nothing, as the less-well-financed private owners soon discovered!

This was a period, of course, in which Ford's personnel changed completely, and rapidly. Director Stuart Turner retired at the end of 1990, Peter Ashcroft succeeded him but retired at the end of 1991, his successor being Colin Dobinson, experienced at Ford but an 'outsider' to the world of rallying, and known as a formidably efficient marketing personality and business manager.

At the same time, chief rally engineer John Wheeler moved away from Boreham, to Dunton, in 1990 to usher the Escort RS Cosworth road car into production, his place at Boreham being taken by his one-time

... and this was Malcolm's way of showing just how well it handled!

Colin Dobinson had taken over from Peter Ashcroft at Boreham in 1992, and headed the 'works' team in the Escort RS Cosworth's first full season, 1993.

deputy Philip Dunabin. Ex-rally-driver John Taylor became the rally service supremo – and would soon move further up the scale.

For 1993 the same 'works' drivers were retained – a really cosmopolitan line-up, with François Delecour of France and Miki Biasion of Italy as regulars, with Malcolm Wilson joining in at times, and regularly running in the British series.

Delecour had been the Sierra driving star since 1991, while ex-double-World-Champion Biasion had moved across from Lancia in 1992. As it happened, and to the surprise of almost everyone, the mercurial Delecour was always the most effective, for Biasion never seemed to show much aggression in these cars – it was almost as if he had decided to coast towards a well-paid retirement.

There was a bigger emphasis on testing and development, and to match this the Boreham facility itself was transformed. The workshops were renovated and re-jigged, almost F1 style, other workshops once used by Ford's truck development department were absorbed and utilized, while the design, purchasing and administrative offices were all relocated to larger, ex-truck, buildings.

Not only that, but within a few years Ford sold the rights to gravel extraction under the surface, so Boreham airfield itself began to look different – and the Essex police also housed a traffic surveillance/rapid response helicopter in the middle of the complex!

Rally car preparation of a 1993-spec Escort RS Cosworth, featuring a very rigid roll cage and a repositioned bag fuel tank.

INTO BATTLE

With sporting homologation achieved on 1 January 1993 (more than 3,000 Escort RS Cosworth road cars had already been produced), rallying began at once. The FIA, for sure, could not complain that this homologation process was a sham – Escort RS Cosworths seemed to be *everywhere*!

Ford's contracted engine builders, Mountune of Maldon, had spent ages improving the YB engine. Although Escort RS Cosworths were now obliged to run with a 38mm restrictor, they had a turbocharger better matched to the engine itself, and could run with a reliable 360bhp at 6,500rpm. (When this figure was first 'leaked' in mid-1993, there was much consternation at Ford, on the grounds that FISA still believed that all 'works' Group A cars were running with 'about 300bhp'. High hopes, or innocence? In later years, we learnt that Lancia and Toyota both had even more power!)

With Mobil and Michelin backing, Boreham planned a ten-event assault on the World Championship in 1993, while private owners' cars were soon ready for European and national series all over the world. To back a two-car 'works' team, Boreham regularly fielded fifteen service vans, two trucks, a communications aircraft, and more than 100 people. By Ford's standards, this was huge spending, though even that was dwarfed by the effort displayed by teams such as Toyota!

Ford might very well have won the Monte in 1993, except that a disbelieving Delecour was passed by an astonishingly fast Toyota on the last stages. How? No-one ever found out, but there rumours of illegal 'rocket fuel' being used, and the same team was later thrown out of the World series for a full year when it was found to be cheating in other ways.

Victories soon followed, however – in Portugal, where Delecour and Biasion beat everyone, to give Ford its first World Championship rally victory since 1981, then in Corsica where a pair of new 'tarmac lightweights' annihilated everyone else (including Toyota – satisfying, that), after which Miki Biasion won the Acropolis.

The rest of the season, in fairness, could not quite go on like this, yet Biasion was

This was the lightweight, magnesium, semi-trailing arm rear suspension assembly used on Group A Escort RS Cosworths in 1993, where the toe-in/toe-out and the camber settings were both adjustable. This was a development of that already used in the 'works' Sierra Cosworth 4×4s.

second in Argentina, Delecour second in New Zealand and third in Australia, before private-owner Franco Cunico won in San Remo, and Delecour once again triumphed in Catalunya/Spain.

Five victories in their first season! All this helped Ford and Delecour take second place in their respective Championships – a performance backed up by eighteen privateer victories in European Championship events – which was wonderful for the first season, specially as private owners also gave Ford victory in the Group N Championship category, too.

For 1994 it was the mixture as before – at least on the surface – although during the year the 'works' team would use a sequential-change gearbox for the first time, 18in wheels put in an appearance, as did the machine-gun sounding anti-lag engine fuelling system being adopted by all serious teams.

Although 1994 started with a bang, when Delecour's Escort RS Cosworth won the Monte Carlo rally – it was Ford's first Monte

The start of a fabulously successful 'works' 1993 season – two brand new Group A cars, their drivers and the service support team, before the start of the Monte Carlo rally. Left to right, in the front row, are Miki Biasion, Tiziano Siviero, Colin Dobinson, John Wheeler, François Delecour and Daniel Grataloup.

François Delecour took second place on the 1993 Monte, having led until the last night. To this day, there are suggestions of sharp practice among his rivals.

win since 1953, and for François it made up for the bitter memories of 1991 and 1993 – the second season was not as excitingly successful as the first. The fact that François broke both his ankles in a non-rallying accident didn't help – for he was then out of the sport for four months.

Even so, a young man called Tommi Makinen won the 1,000 Lakes rally in his only Ford 'works' drive (he then moved to Mitsubishi, and had won four Drivers' Championships by the end of the 1990s!), and there were minor placings galore, including a quartet of third places in Portugal, Argentina, San Remo and the RAC events. This was the year in which Ford finished third in the Manufacturers' series, and in which Ford once again won the Group N category.

There were no fewer than twenty-nine outright victories in European Championship events (few other manufacturers have ever been able to boast results like that), while Malcolm Wilson's Michelin-Pilot-sponsored cars so completely dominated the British Championship that the regulations were speedily changed to eliminate the Escort RS Cosworth in future!

In the meantime there was turmoil at Boreham. Not only had Colin Dobinson moved on, his place being taken up by ex Ford Australia

personality Peter Gillitzer, but also there was a period when the World rallying effort was due to be closed down. Money, or the lack of it, was behind this shock. Such a decision was announced in July, and it was not until the very end of the season that this stance was changed.

During the season, too, 'works' driver Miki Biasion's form had been disappointing, and although he blamed the car and the team for this, and his Latin temperament didn't help, Ford management took the opposite view, and dropped him at the end of the 1994 season. Like Italian red wine, it seems, he had not 'travelled' as well as hoped, and had only won one event in his three-year stay.

Although Gillitzer somehow got the 'close-down' decision reversed, it was at the expense of budget and commitment. Determined to keep Ford in rallying, in F1 *and* in Touring Car racing, all at the same time, he had had to spread his available funds too thinly.

The result was that although Boreham remained in being, RAS Sport of Belgium took on part of the effort (and prepared their own cars). François Delecour, still Ford's lead driver, had to be joined by the cheerful Belgian Bruno Thiry, and although there was still a commitment to improving the car, this process slowed down.

Most of the year's innovation came in the transmission, where the sequential gearchange system of 1994 was abandoned, a six-speed gearbox took over from the original seven-speeder (same casing, different cluster), and active centre differentials were also specified. That, and constant minor changes to the engines improved the cars by the end of the season – but made them no more successful.

Called RAS-Ford throughout the year, splitting the effort (and producing odd-looking cars with fragmented sponsorship) might have saved money but it did not produce enough results. Although Delecour took second place in Monte Carlo and in Corsica, plus a fourth place in Spain, Thiry was not so lucky. Highest-placed of the two drivers on more than one occasion, he led the Tour de Corse until just two stages from the finish, when a wheel bearing collapsed and stranded him a long way from service.

There was bad luck everywhere, it seemed – for Delecour might also have won in Monte Carlo if a shock absorber had not broken on the final night.

Miki Biasion won the gruelling Acropolis rally of 1993, the 'works' car's first outright victory on truly rough roads.

Elsewhere, the Escort RS Cosworth was still very successful, with twenty-five outright victories in European Rally Championship rounds, dominating in the UK, and also winning the Mitropa, Austrian, Bulgarian, Swiss, Danish, Estonian, French, Finnish, Italian, Irish, Norwegian, Dutch, Portuguese, Slovakian and Turkish series, too!

SWANSONG

Morale was desperately low at the end of 1995, not least because the real rallying enthusiasts at Boreham believed their bosses were no longer committed, or simply didn't understand what rallying was all about.

This, though, was to be a season of miraculous rebirths. Not only was all preparation and operation brought back in-house to Boreham (where John Taylor was Operations Manager and he, at least, knew his stuff), but twice World Champion Carlos Sainz was signed on a two-year contract – and the cars started winning again.

It was a new-look team – Carlos brought Repsol sponsorship with him, which meant that the cars were painted in a new red and white livery – and the atmosphere was different. Delecour left the team after the Swedish (his form, post-accident, had been disappointing), after which Bruno Thiry took his place.

The season started with a real surprise. Monte Carlo was not an official World Championship round in 1996, so Boreham did not send any cars. No matter. In their place Patrick Bernardini of Corsica won outright in a privately-prepared car (co-driven by Bernard Occelli, who usually sat with Didier Auriol), at his very first attempt!

Throughout the season Sainz, aided, abetted and (most importantly) cherished by John Taylor, made his mark with the Escort. Second in Sweden (by only twenty-three seconds), he then won in Indonesia. Third in the Acropolis, second in Argentina, third in Australia and once again second in San Remo (by just twenty-two seconds), Carlos showed that the Escort was still a force. He, like the team, finished a strong third in the World Series.

As before, the Escort was still a winner all over the world, with twenty-four victories at European Championship level, victory for Mohammed Bin Sulayem in the prestigious Middle East series, success in the Central European, and a host of wins at national level.

This, though, was almost the end of the road for the 'works' RS Cosworth – as a new derivative, the Escort World Rally Car, was on the way.

'WORKS' RS2000s – FRONT-WHEEL-DRIVE F2 CARS

Although the factory team had little time to spend on the lesser Escorts, it encouraged Gordon Spooner Engineering to evolve a Group A version of the 16-valve RS2000 for use in what was becoming known as the 'Formula 2' category. Although this started out as a laudable attempt to contain costs (the FIA even promoted a separate World Championship for such cars), it failed. Within two years an 'F2' RS2000 was as special, in its own way, as the Escort RS Cosworth had already become.

RS2000 development started modestly in 1993, when Gwyndaf Evans took a Vecta-sponsored car to win the Group N category (and third place, overall) of the British Rally Championship.

Then, for 1994, Gwyndaf moved up to the new Group A 'F2' category, with a 'works'-backed car having at least 225bhp and a six-speed transmission. Early-season troubles were worrying, but in the Lombard-RAC rally the latest GSE-built car was effective; Gwyndaf not only won the 'F2' category, but also finished seventh overall – behind six full-house four-wheel-drive monsters, three of which were 'works' Escort RS Cosworths.

To promote front-wheel-drive 2ltr rallying even further, for 1995 the FIA brought in a new 'Kit Car' formula, which allowed more

François Delecour won the Rally of Spain in October 1993 – this being the fourth World Championship rally win for a Boreham car during the year.

engine and chassis freedom. Although Ford did not actively get involved internationally in this, the RS2000 was still a competitive prospect in Britain.

In the British Rally Championship, where points scoring (though not individual event victories – confusing!) was confined to front-wheel-drive F2 cars, Gwyndaf Evans' cars, once again prepared by Gordon Spooner Engineering and now with at least 240bhp, were always on the pace. Second in the over-all Championship, Gwyndaf finished second overall on the Manx (beaten only by an Escort RS Cosworth!).

Not only that, but on the Lombard-RAC rally at the end of the season, this Rapid Fit-sponsored car again won the F2 category, and finished sixth overall – beaten only by three 'works' Subaru Imprezas and two Escort RS Cosworths!

In 1996, once again Ford made no attempt to send the RS2000 out into the wide world to contest major F2 events, but backed several cars – most notably for Gwyndaf Evans – for the British series. In new Group A machines, sponsored by Response Computers, Gwyndaf rewarded them with two outright victories

and two second places in the F2 category – and won the Championship outright.

Although Gwyndaf got a new wide-track, flared arch, 282bhp 'Kit Car' RS2000 before the end of the season, he could not quite repeat that trick in 1997, though he had two second places and two third places, finishing fourth overall in the British series. High-speed accidents in Cumbria (the Pirelli) and the Manx rather spoiled his season.

This, though, was the high-point for the front-wheel-drive Ford, as Gwyndaf was then tempted away by a good offer from SEAT, and no-one could really replace him. The Sim-monite sisters made plenty of headlines in their Ladies' Championship programmes, but there were never truly competitive.

WORLD RALLY CAR – FOR A SPECIAL PURPOSE

Even while the Escort RS Cosworth was at its peak, world rallying's authorities were formulating yet another set of rules. Some manufacturers wanting to break into rally-ing were not prepared to develop special

1994, and no Monte mistake for François Delecour, who won the event after failing so closely in 1993.

four-wheel-drive models and then build at least 2,500 of them. To them, Group A was now seen as a closed shop.

Intensive lobbying then followed, the result being the birth of what became known as World Rally Cars. Although only twenty such machines had to be built in one season (none for use as road cars), they had to be based on models of which at least 25,000 cars (such as front-wheel-drive Escorts) were being made in a year.

Conversion to four-wheel drive was authorized, engines (which could be enlarged, or sleeved down) had to be no more than 2ltr in capacity, and the cars had to be at least 157in (4m) in length.

It didn't take much thought to see that a WRC (as these machines were immediately known) could be made much more specialized, and much more effective, even than the best Group A cars. Though the Escort RS Cosworth was still ultra-competitive as a Group A car, from 1 January 1997, when WRC rules took over at top level, it would be rendered obsolete.

But Ford immediately sensed a big problem. Investment in an all-new WRC would cost millions, and could only really be justified by using the new model for several years. Yet the replacement for the existing Escort – the Focus – was due to be launched in 1998.

Ford, therefore, consulted the FIA, explained their problem, assured them that building an all-new Focus-based WRC was out of the question until 1999, and suggested an interim solution. If its first-generation WRC could be based on the Escort RS Cosworth (which was, itself, based on the Escort), then it could be on the starting line for Monte Carlo in January 1997. If not – well, they would simply be obliged to withdraw from rallying until 1999.

Although the FIA agreed (Ford, in fact, was the *only* manufacturer granted this

Monte victory at last for Ford – in 1994, and 41 years after the previous success. François Delecour (right) and Daniel Grataloup celebrate their success.

concession), the rush to get a viable WRC ready was considerable. Concept work started in June 1996, the first prototype was completed on 13 October, the first tests were completed a week later, the car was unveiled on 3 November, and homologation inspection of the twenty necessary kits of parts was completed on 19 December! It never gets much quicker than that.

The temptation to make a comparison with the gestation of the Escort RS Cosworth – well over four years from original concept to homologation – is inescapable. This time around, with no road-car development, or legal legislation and homologation to worry about, the Escort WRC went

Bruny Thiry drove this works-prepared Escort RS Cosworth into sixth place in the 1994 Monte.

from 'Good Idea' to homologation in seven months!

This, incidentally, is one good reason why thoughts of developing an Escort-based WRC with a new-generation Zetec engine (as later to be used in the Focus WRC), or even to consider using a V6-engined Mondeo, were both abandoned, not only because of development risks, but mainly because of the time factor.

As Engineering Manager Philip Dunabin commented at the time of launch:

> Our request to the FIA to base the World Rally Car on the existing Escort 4×4 has allowed us to build a long-term plan on the existing and future Escort models ... the decision to base the World Rally Car on the current Escort was never really questioned.

The phrase 'future Escort models' passed almost without comment, for the development of such a new Ford model was already very much of an open secret. The fact that this eventually became the 'Focus' was not hidden in 1996, as that name would not actually be adopted until 1998.

IMPROVEMENTS

How much did all this cost? Ford has never released a figure, but by most previous standards it must have been very little indeed. Time, not money, was the enemy in 1996, for there was one inescapable target which could not be missed – two cars had to be on the start line of the Monte Carlo rally in January 1997.

Led by Philip Dunabin, Ford Motorsport looked at their existing state-of-the-art Escort RS Cosworth rally car (*not* the road car, of course) to search for improvements.

François Delecour won the non-championship PTV rally of 1994 in his ex-1993 Spanish winning car.

Escort World Rally Car (1996–1998)

Layout
Unit construction steel body/chassis structure. Two-door plus hatchback, front engine/four-wheel drive, sold as two-seater sports hatchback, purely for rallying.

Engine
Type	Ford-Cosworth YB series
Block material	Cast iron
Head material	Cast aluminium
Cylinders	4 in-line
Cooling	Water
Bore and stroke	90.82×76.95mm
Capacity	1,993cc
Main bearings	5
Valves	4 per cylinder, directly operated by twin overhead camshafts, via inverted bucket-type tappets, with the camshafts driven by cogged belt from the crankshaft
Compression ratio	9.6:1 (Nominal)
Fuel supply	Ford Pectel fuel injection, with IHI turbocharger
Max power	300bhp @ 5,500rpm
Max torque	434lb ft at 4,000rpm

Transmission
Six-speed manual gearbox, non-synchromesh, and four-wheel-drive incorporating variable front/rear torque split and 'active' differentials

Clutch	Diaphragm spring

Suspension and steering
Front	Independent, by coil springs, MacPherson struts, track control arms, and anti-roll bar
Rear	Independent, by coil springs, MacPherson struts, track control arms, anti-roll bar
Steering	Rack-and-pinion, with power assistance
Tyres	Various: 16in, 17in, 18in radial-ply
Wheels	Cast alloy disc, bolt-on fixing
Rim width	Various

Brakes
Type	Disc brakes at front, discs at rear, hydraulically operated, with no ABS anti-lock control
Size	(Typically) Tarmac: 14.9in front discs, 12.3in rear discs. Gravel: 12.4in front discs, 12.4in rear discs

Dimensions (in/mm)
Track	
Front	60.2/1,530
Rear	60.2/1,530

Wheelbase	100.4/2,551
Overall length	165.8/4,211
Overall width	69.7/1,770
Overall height	56.1/1,425
Unladen weight	2,712lb/1,230kg

UK retail price
Special order, price depending on specification and extra parts ordered

The list, as revealed by Ford, was long on detail, and can be summarized as follows:

Engine: New (smaller, to suit a 34mm restrictor) IHI turbocharger, different exhaust manifold, and fuel injection changes (with eight instead of four active injectors). This, we now know, resulted in a peak power output of 310bhp at 5,500rpm, and a very solid torque curve, even more meaty than it had been with the previous, larger, restrictor.
Cooling: Better airflow through larger front apertures, with relocated intercooler and water radiators.
Rear suspension: Lighter and stronger tubular sub-frame, supporting new-style MacPherson strut/links system, with a geometry rather like that of the Mondeo.
Aerodynamics: New front bumper profile. Smaller/reshaped rear aerofoil to generate more downforce with less drag.
Weight distribution: Further idealized, with 80ltr fuel tank, spare wheel, and 40ltr water reservoir (for cooling sprays) centrally positioned in the rear compartment.

Aerodynamic improvements were pursued in the Ford wind-tunnel at Merkenich, following initial suggestions by Nigel Stroud of Reynard, these resulting in improved front *and* rear downforce. The new aerofoil was necessary, in any case, to meet the regulations: the Escort RS Cosworth style of spoiler was too large to pass through the

Gwyndaf Evans driving the Vecta-sponsored Group N Escort RS Cosworth to a category success in the 1993 Ulster Rally.

Two very important Ford Motorsport personalities – Stuart Turner (right) and Carlos Sainz.

François Delecour drove this Repsol-sponsored Escort RS Cosworth in the 1996 Swedish Rally.

Carlo Sainz's finest performance in an Escort World Rally Car was to win the 1997 Acropolis rally, with team mate Juha Kankkunen (seen here) just 17 seconds behind him.

'template' imposed by new WRC regulations.

At the front, these changes were all connected with the need to package a 33 per cent larger water radiator, and the fitment of a 50 per cent larger turbo intercooler (which was additionally cooled by water spray from the reservoir behind the front seats) ahead, rather than on top of, that radiator.

MORE CHANGES

Then came the really big gamble. It was enough of a challenge to developing a new car, but Motorsport Director Martin Whitaker (who had taken over from Peter Gillitzer in mid-1996) also elected to change the way the team was run. For 1997, and for the very first time in Ford's history, the 'works' cars would be run by an outside agency.

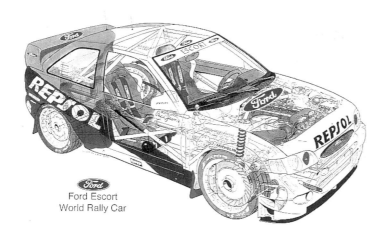

The Escort World Rally Car of 1997–98 was the ultimate rallying Escort, complete with MacPherson strut type rear suspension.

Ford Escort
World Rally Car

Because Carlos Sainz had left the team, taking his Repsol sponsorship with him, the 1998 'works' team ran in Ford corporate colours.

At the end of 1996, therefore, Boreham closed its doors on World Championship motorsport (permanently, as it transpired), and Malcolm Wilson's M-Sport team, based near Cockermouth, in Cumbria, took over. Boreham takes the credit for the design and development of the Escort WRC, and for the hurried manufacture of the first twenty sets of components, but it was Malcolm Wilson's team which would always run the cars.

Boreham stalwarts like John Taylor and Robin Vokins were no longer seen around the world. Instead the 'works' team would be run by Malcolm Wilson, with ex-Mitsubishi Ralliart engineer Marc Amblard as his engineer.

There were driver changes, too. Carlos Sainz led the team, but for the first part of 1997 he was joined by the German, Armin Schwarz. Unhappily, sponsorship promised by Schwarz as part of his package never appeared, so from mid-season he was dropped, and replaced by four-times World Rally Champion Juha Kankkunen.

Visually the change was in the shape of the cars, for the Repsol sponsor's colour scheme was much as it had been with the last of the Escort RS Cosworths in 1996. The only real difference (Ford found this recurringly expensive) was that these cars showed a distressing tendency to shed their massive front bumper/spoilers in water-splashes – not only embarrassing (and exposing the radiator/intercooler packaging) but expensive, as these were made from a carbon fibre-based material.

With world rallying finally settling on to a fourteen-event format, where in F1 style the top teams had to compete in every rally to qualify for points to be scored, the car build, preparation, repair and refurbishment routine was always going to be intense. There were those who suggested that M-Sport would simply not get the job done. But it did!

Somehow (but even today, he isn't quite sure how), M-Sport managed to get two brand-new cars (P6 FMC and P7 FMC) to the start line in Monte Carlo, and were able to use the same two cars again in Sweden a few weeks later. The rest of the season, Malcolm admitted, was always a relentless race against time, but by using no more than nine separate cars during the year, the team made it.

Juha Kankkunen was Ford's most successful driver in the 1998 World Rally Championship, taking third in the Swedish rally (this event), and fourth in the overall drivers' series.

Technical advances during the year were in detail, not in concept, these including changes to the differentials, with an Xtrac sequential change used from mid-season, and with Hi-Tech dampers replacing Dynamic types from mid-season.

1997 was a season in which Ford came so close to the ultimate glory – where the team finished second in the Makes Championship, and the ever-consistent Sainz took third place in the Drivers' series. Carlos himself won in the Acropolis and in Indonesia, with second places in Monte Carlo, Sweden, the Tour de Corse and New Zealand: not only that, but in Corsica he was foiled by a mere eight seconds, in New Zealand by thirteen seconds, and in Sweden by sixteen seconds. Juha Kankkunen, who joined the team in May, recorded no fewer than four second places (twice finishing close behind Sainz, with team orders applied).

During the season, no fewer than twenty-nine Escort WRCs were built and rallied at World level – ten of those being updates/conversions from previously-rallied Escort RS Cosworths – this proving that Ford had never had problems in utilising the twenty sets of parts which had been

Hello and goodbye! At the end of 1998, Ford posed the last of the 'works' Escorts against a mockup of the forthcoming Focus WRC cars.

Gwyndaf Evans (right) and Howard Davies used Escort RS2000s to win the British Rally Championship in 1996.

lined up for display in the previous December.

Privately-owned WRCs rallied in various European countries, most notably where Patrick Snyers' Bastos-backed Belgian car won several ERC events.

For 1998 the entire rallying world, it seemed, knew that the Escort WRC would be starting its second, and last, World Championship campaign. Months before the road car was even previewed, M-Sport started work on the design of its Focus WRC (a car which would share nothing with the Escort), and after this there was really little further development on the Escort WRC.

The team, in fact, started the new season with a different turbocharger housing, which helped to provide a more powerful engine, and the cars were now so light that they needed ballast to run at the minimum weight imposed by regulations. Electronic 'launch control' of the engines was used to give even more effective starts from the beginning of special stages.

Carlos Sainz had left the team (but he would be back – in 2000), being replaced as team leader by Juha Kankkunen, the second driver (as in some events in 1996) being

Driving this Rapid Fit-sponsored RS2000, Gwyndaf Evans won the 'Formula 2' category of the RAC rally in 1994.

Bruno Thiry. Because the Repsol sponsorship was from Spain, this followed Sainz to his new team (Toyota), so the 1998 Fords looked very different – blue and white, with a Ford 'Blue Oval' much in evidence.

This time, in its final 'works' season, the Escort finished fourth in the World Rally Championship, but there were no outright victories. Juha Kankkunen, fourth in the Drivers Championship, took three second places, and was third four times more, but Thiry could only record one third place – on the RAC Rally of Great Britain.

It was fitting and nostalgic but, above all, sad that the 'works' Escort team should start its last event on home ground. Second and third places overall in the Rally of Great Britain was the very best which could be expected of this ageing design – and one should also note that Sebastian Lindholm (in a privately-entered Escort WRC) took fifth place, while Schwarz's car finished seventh. No other marque was so well placed.

For the record, no fewer than nineteen Escort WRCs appeared in the 1998 World Championship season, of which only four had previously featured in 1997, and of which only nine different cars were official M-Sport entries. When a number of private conversions, which appeared in lesser events throughout the season, are added in to the total, this brings the total of Escort WRCs built in two years to well over fifty.

In Cheltenham, therefore, in November 1998 the rallying career of the 'works' Escorts was brought proudly to a close, thirty years and seven months after it had begun in San Remo, Italy in March 1968.

This was a period in which countless – tens of thousands, certainly – rallies, rallysprints and rallycross events had been won by one or other of the Escort family. It was a breed of car which had brought success, sparkle, excitement and glamour to motorsport all over the world – and in my opinion no other such rally car has ever been built.

High flying! Gwyndaf Evans/Howard Davies in their 'F2' Escort RS2000 on the 1996 Manx rally, on their way to becoming British rally champions.

In July 1998, as Boreham was about to lose its prominence as a motorsport centre, a massive staff reunion was held in Bill Meade's garden. Among the well-known personalities present were Stuart Turner, Bill Barnett, Barry Lee, Tony Mason, Gordon Spooner, Terry Hoyle, John Griffiths, John Taylor, Mick Jones, Boreham secretary Pam Goater, and several of the 'works' mechanics.

11 Escort RS2000 and 4×4 – 16 Valves for the 1990s

Even before it went on sale in the summer of 1990, the new-generation Escort became controversial. A high-performance version, the RS2000, though not yet ready for sale, was being damned before anyone had even seen it.

So, what had gone wrong? Ford, after all, had spent at least £1,000 million, and four years, on it. Maybe it was because Ford hadn't been bold in any of its features – in styling, in engineering, in marketing or in pricing. Maybe it was because the new cars didn't have enough 'character'. And maybe, somehow, it was if the world's media had fallen out of love with Ford for a time, and decided to give them a hard time.

There's no question, though, that when the new cars (which were unofficially,

though never actually advertised as such, the Mk V range) appeared, they were seen as disappointing. Although everyone agreed that they were an improvement on the 1980s-generation which they replaced (particularly in their packaging), they were not *that* much better. The problem was that they didn't seem to be market leaders in any way – this being a moment when other rivals looked better, were technically more advanced, handled better, and were often cheaper.

Not that the buying public seemed to mind too much, as the new car shot to the head of the sales charts at once, and stayed there for a long time in the 1990s. Once again, it seemed, public response was very

Little things mean a lot – the RS2000 of 1991 used the same basic body style of the mainstream Escort, but with two bonnet bulges, special alloy wheels and a big front spoiler.

187

The 1990s-style RS2000 not only had a rear spoiler, and five-spoke alloy wheels, but a discreet little badge on the hatchback.

This was the original fascia / instrument panel layout of the 1990s-style RS2000, naturally coming with Recaro seats as standard.

different from that of the media, and Escort production was all set to be measured in millions – so as a business project it was clearly set to be a success.

16-VALVE NOVELTY

In 1990, though, there was no immediate RS model in the new range – although Ford certainly made the promise of a new car appearing within the next year. The out-going Mk IV range, of course, had been flag-shipped by the 105bhp XR3i and the 132bhp Escort RS Turbo types – both of them with versions of the single-cam/8-valve CVH engine – but neither re-appeared in the new range in 1990. The most sporty to be offered at first was the 108bhp/1.6ltr CVH engine for the Escort S and the Cabriolet – and it seemed that turbocharging had been dismissed to the heritage cupboard.

But there was hope. Even in August 1990, Ford revealed that two new RS models were already on the way – the Escort RS Cosworth (previewed, in spectacular but premature condition, at the launch – *see* Chapter 9), and an RS2000. But the Escort RS Cosworth would not be ready until 1992, while first deliveries of the RS2000 were promised during 1991.

As before, 'RS2000' indicated a car with a 2,000cc engine, but this time it was to be with a unique, never-been-seen-before 16-valve twin-cam engine.

But what was the RS2000 to be? Although its specification was only partly revealed at the time, this third-generation car, an RS2000 for the '90s, looked very promising. The basic facts told their own story, and an instant comparison between new and old, separated by more than a decade, is instructive:

RS2000	**RS2000**
1991 model	Late-1970s
Mk V	Mk II
Layout	
Front-wheel-drive	Rear-wheel-drive
Transverse engine	In-line engine
Hatchback	Saloon
Engine	
16-valve I4	8-valve Pinto
150bhp	110bhp
Transmission	
5-speed	4-speed
Suspension	
All-independent	Beam rear axle
Top speed (mph)	
131	108

And there were even rumours (whispers, and behind-the-hand hints, really) of a possible four-wheel-drive version. For the moment,

The RS2000's 16-valve engine was all-new in 1991, with a torquey fuel-injected 150bhp layout.

though, RS dealers had nothing to sell, and enthusiasts could only wait.

More than a year after the new-generation Escort had been introduced, the RS2000 finally appeared in the autumn of 1991 – and the wait was seen to be worthwhile. Although there were few style changes to differentiate this special model from the others, as a package there was complete transformation.

Transformation? Certainly – and I can personally vouch for this. Having driven the ordinary Escorts in 1990, I was puzzled at the characterless enigma that lay behind their behaviour. Then, having driven prototype RS2000s far and fast along German autobahns a year later, I was electrified.

Astonishment came at once. Surging away from the factory venue was one thing, but joining a limit-free autobahn, and being able to outpace almost everything, was something else. Up to 100–110mph (160–177km/h) was no problem (and most traffic on German autobahns drove at least as quickly as that in those days), but the ability to surge up to 120mph (193km/h) was quite a new experience.

Not only that, but here was a new-generation Escort which also steered, handled, and felt like a true hot hatchback should – and it was fair to say that the only imponderable, at the time, was what it might cost.

That was a day on which many BMW and Mercedes-Benz drivers must have been puzzled: normally they would have blown off this type of Escort, elbowing it into the near-side lane with contemptuous ease – but here was a new type that gave them trouble. Not only that, but when we turned off into the twisting and hilly territory west of Cologne, we found that the handling was a revelation. Gathering back at base afterwards, there was a real buzz in the air.

As David Vivian later wrote in *Autocar & Motor*:

> No one knows better than Ford how to turn a humdrum car into a humdinger. Witness

the miracles of the past: the Mk I Escort RS1600, the Capri RS3100, the Sierra RS Cosworth. Great cars, all of them. And all derived from high-volume cookers which, if accidentally locked out of, you wouldn't necessarily want to get back into.

The common theme here, of course, is 'RS', Rallye Sport ... Ford's competition record positively shimmers with success, and data gathered on the track has been applied adroitly ...

All true, of course, but in this case the miracle was that it had been achieved with little reference to Ford's Special Vehicle Engineering department. Here, for the very first time, was an RS-badged car which had been engineered by Ford's mainstream engineers at Dunton and Cologne.

Not that the original cars, as designed, were as good as this. One day at Boreham in 1991, various motorsport personalities were invited to drive a prototype, and I heard their comments afterwards. At that time, incidentally, the new car rejoiced in the unimaginative name for European sale of 'XR Plus', which might explain why its behaviour was not acceptable.

For 1992 the RS2000 used this very laid-back style, but there was 150bhp and a five-speed box under the bonnet, and the top speed was almost 130mph (210km/h).

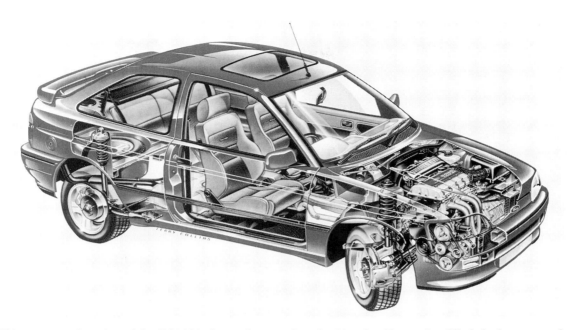

This cutaway drawing of the RS2000 shows the way that the 16-valve 2ltr engine filled the bonnet, and also shows the four-wheel disc braking layout and the all-round strut suspension.

Gwyndaf Evans, not only an accomplished rally driver but a Ford dealer himself, apparently said that it was still not the sort of car which had handling worthy of the RS badge, and that he personally would not like to have to sell it like that. Along with other similar remarks, his views were noted, SVE was consulted, and the production car was considerably improved.

When the first cars were ready for delivery in November 1991, Ford was proud of what had been achieved. The British TV commercial featured an experienced Ford design engineer digging out a cob-webby RS2000 Mk II from the depths of his garage (actually this was a cunningly 'aged' concourse-condition car which Ford had borrowed from an RSOC member), repeatedly improving the performance of a new-style car, seeing it drive up the steps of Philadelphia's City Hall in the USA (no, I don't know why either) where, to the sound-track of a *Rocky* movie, the tag line was, quite simply: 'The Champ is Back'.

Stirring stuff, but at £15,995 in the UK, would it sell?

TRANSFORMATION SCENE

Let's get the visual improvements lined up straight away. Starting from the rather plain-Jane looks of the latest three-door hatchback Escort, for the new RS2000 Ford had included a deep new front spoiler, a simple hatchback lid spoiler, special six-spoke wide-rim cast alloy wheels, and twin 'power-bulges' in the bonnet. Ford's famous tilt-and-slide sun roof was standard. It wasn't much, but it was enough: that package, and the tailgate badge, told its own story.

191

All RS2000s were three-door types, being much smoother and more user-friendly than the much-loved 1970s variety.

Because it ran on a 99.4in (2,525mm) wheelbase, this was a roomier car than any previous RS2000, and the rounded body style hid an extremely capable chassis. By 1990s standards the transverse engine and 'end-on' gearbox layout was conventional enough, but both were brand new.

Front and rear suspensions – MacPherson strut and 'twist beam' respectively – were merely up-rated versions of those used in other Escorts of this family (and the strongly-related new-type Fiesta), but this was the only early-1990s Escort with four-wheel disc brakes, electronic ABS brakes and power-assisted steering as standard – and an up-market interior where the latest Recaro front seats got pride of place.

The engine itself was a revelation. This was the very first design of four-valves-per-cylinder Ford twin-cam unit which had needed no technical input from Cosworth – and was the very first Ford 16-valver to be manufactured in-house. Ford's own engineers had evolved this unit all on their own

– and with a run-all-day rating of 150bhp at 6,000rpm, it was magnificent.

As with so many components to be found in Escort RS models, here was a 'building block' with a history. In the beginning there had been a new-generation engine (coded 'I4'), a two-valves-per-cylinder 2ltr twin-cam, which had been designed for use in the Sierra, Scorpio and (yes, you'd better believe it!) in the Transit van.

The 8-valve I4, with chain-driven overhead camshafts, had first been unveiled in May 1989. Rated at 109bhp (with a Weber carburettor) and 125bhp (with fuel injection), it was manufactured at Dagenham (Ford claimed they had invested £157 million to make it so), and displaced the aged single-cam Pinto in several ranges almost at once.

I should make it clear that this I4 engine family had nothing in common with the old Pinto (except, that is, that it was a four-cylinder unit!): not only were the bore and stroke dimensions both different, but it had a shorter and more squat cylinder block, the length saving being 2.4in (61mm).

The RS2000 of 1991 had a narrow-angle 16-valve twin-cam engine, with cam drive by chain. Cosworth inspiration? Not this time – it was a completely in-house design.

Not only did I4 have a lighter yet much more rigid cylinder block, but it used an aluminium cylinder head, its twin overhead camshafts were driven by chain (not by a cogged belt) – and it was suitably packaged for 'in-line' *or* 'transverse' installation.

The 16-valve version came later, and was originally intended only for use in cars like the RS2000, as it was not thought refined or smooth enough for cars like the Sierra Ghia and the Scorpio. Naturally it had to meet all existing, and threatened, exhaust emissions regulations, but it had to pass all of Ford's fearsome endurance tests. To do this, there was Ford's EECIV fuel injection/engine management system to control the fuel supply, along with a catalytic convertor (the first on a Ford RS model) in the system to clean up the exhaust fumes.

Because it produced 75bhp/ltr, by any standards this was Ford's most efficient engine so far – and Ford made sure that everyone knew that it was all their own work. With a fat torque curve (as a long-time owner of RS2000s, I can guarantee all this) it made the car easy to drive, and there was absolutely no temperament, no flat-spots – and no sudden falling away of power at the top end.

And not only did it feel good, but it looked the part, too. When one opened up the bonnet, the reason for one of the power bulges was obvious. The polished aluminium camshaft drive sprocket cover on the right side of the car always came perilously close to making contact with the metal pressing, so a bulge had been added to make that clearance more comfortable – but the other bulge was there just to provide symmetry! The logo 'DOHC 2000 16V' was proudly displayed on a red cover along the top of the cylinder head. Here was an engine that meant business – and it showed.

The five-speed gearbox was also a surprise, and another innovation. Not merely an update of the old 'B5' transmission used in the last of the Escort RS Turbos (which was not sturdy enough to accept the 140lb ft torque of the new 16-valve I4), this was the larger, sturdier, brand-new MTX75 unit which had an important future at Ford.

Already planned as a cornerstone of the Sierra-replacement range (the front-wheel-drive Mondeo, which was not due to be revealed until 1993), Ford's planners made sure that the first machining and assembly lines for the MTX75 transmission came on stream early at Cologne, and the RS2000 benefited from it. Not only was this box absolutely right for Ford's new hot hatch, but this was an ideal way of shaking out the problems before Mondeo assembly began: there were few.

Escort RS2000 (1991–1996)

Layout
Unit construction steel body/chassis structure. Two-door plus hatchback, front engine/front-wheel drive, sold as four-seater sports hatchback.

Engine
Type   Ford I4
Block material   Cast iron
Head material   Cast aluminium
Cylinders   4 in-line
Cooling   Water
Bore and stroke   86.0 × 86.0mm
Capacity   1,998cc
Main bearings   5
Valves   4 per cylinder, directly operated by twin overhead camshafts, via bucket-type hydraulic tappets, with the camshafts driven by chain from the crank-shaft
Compression ratio   10.3:1
Fuel supply   Ford EEC-IV fuel injection
Max power   150bhp @ 6,000rpm (Later re-rated to 148bhp)
Max torque   140lb ft at 4,500rpm

Transmission
Five-speed manual gearbox, all-synchromesh
Clutch   Single plate, diaphragm spring

Overall gearbox ratios
Top   3.247
4th   4.240
3rd   5.654
2nd   8.137
1st   12.339
Reverse   13.217
Final drive   3.82:1
(20.2mph (32.4km/h)/1,000rpm in top gear)

Suspension and steering
Front   Independent, by coil springs, MacPherson struts, track control arms, and anti-roll bar
Rear   Independent, by coil springs, torsion beam axle, trailing arms, anti-roll bar and telescopic dampers
Steering   Rack-and-pinion, with power assistance
Tyres   195/50VR-15in radial-ply
Wheels   Cast alloy disc, bolt-on fixing
Rim width   6.0in

The RS2000's final fascia-style, introduced in early 1995, was a great improvement on the original, with soft curves instead of angles, and a full range of features. The airbag steering wheel was phased in during the winter of 1993–94.

simpler front-wheel-drive machine – but on twisty roads, where ultimate traction mattered, there was no comparison. This car was so capable, and it felt so good, that it could have handled a lot more power.

To quote one pundit:

> Enter a corner slightly too fast in the 4×4 and squeezing on the power in mid-bend merely tightens your chosen cornering line. Do the same in the front-wheel-drive car and you would have to come off the power to adjust your cornering line.
>
> Quite simply, the RS2000 4×4 is more efficient than its front-drive sibling ...

A DIVERSION

This was the time when a few romantics started harking back to the charismatic rear-drive RS2000s of the 1970s, and wondering why it could not happen again. Why didn't Ford just disconnect the front-wheel

drive shafts of the latest cars, they said, and have done with it?

This, in fact, was quite impractical – but since Ford's SVE engineers had found themselves with a little spare time at this juncture, they were allowed to build a brace of other rear-drive Escorts instead. In both cases they used an Escort RS Cosworth structure and platform – using a 'north-south-' (in-line-) located 16-valve RS2000 engine in one case, and a 24-valve Scorpio V6 engine in the other.

Engines were mated to the rear-drive Sierra type of MT75 gearbox, along with an Escort RS Cosworth/Sierra RS Cosworth axle and independent rear suspension. After both projects had been abandoned on the 'good fun while it lasted' basis, they were shown in public, though I understand that neither even came close to going into production.

Another diversion was the use later made of modified versions of the RS2000's 16-valve engine. Starting at the end of 1994 Ford refreshed the Scorpio large-car range, notably with a controversial new front-end style, making a 136bhp version of this once-unique RS2000 engine one of its power units.

Because that engine was still not quite refined enough for the Scorpio, in August 1996 it was displaced by a different version – not only was this an enlarged, 145bhp, 2,295cc power unit, but it had been equipped with a pair of chain-driven 'Lanchester' balancer shafts to smooth it out!

The same power unit was later committed, in a transverse front-drive location, as one of the engines available in Ford's versatile seven-seater MPV 'people mover', the Galaxy, this move coming in March 1997.

This transformation – and it felt like that, no less – had been wrought with the help of Cosworth, who had devised an ingenious mounting for the two balancer shafts. In previous rivals' engines, such chain-driven shafts were mounted at the side of the cylinder block, often being positioned in tunnels in re-tooled cylinder blocks.

This was not Cosworth's way, who liked to think laterally (or, in this case, vertically). Realizing that balancer shafts were long and slim, but were not bulky, Cosworth actually placed them in the base of the engine sump, immediately *below* the line of the crankshaft, where they were chain-driven from the nose of the crank. Even more craftily, that chain only drove one balancer shaft gear, both shafts then being geared together, at double engine speed.

Testers loved the result, and the mind boggles at the effect of combining this engineering with a reversion to RS2000-style camshaft timing and tuning details? 165bhp in silky smoothness? Yes, it could have been nice.

FINAL MAKEOVER

Within months of the RS2000 4×4 finally going on sale, there was yet another change to the entire Escort range – the final one, as

From early 1995 to the end of 1996, when it was finally discontinued, the RS2000 used this different, slitty-grille, front-end style.

it happens, and one which was to endure until the last Escort of all was built at Halewood in July 2000.

The third type of 1990s Escort (and the second major facelift in little more than four years) was unquestionably the best, and raised the question – why could not the 1991 models have been as good? One answer, maybe, was that the original cars were developed under a Ford engineering management which was more cost-conscious and less engineering-driven than it should have been – and was eventually discredited – (and for which few personalities now claim credit) while the 1995 version had been strongly influenced by the high-flying engineer Richard Parry-Jones, a driving enthusiast to whom handling seemed to be more important than cost saving!

From early 1995, therefore, every Escort got yet another new nose – this one having different headlamps, a wider, yet slimmer grille profile, and yet another set of new front-end sheet metal pressings, there were smoothly-profiled bumpers at front and rear, and some subtle body stiffening to increase the already impressive rigidity.

Inside the car was a completely new fascia/instrument layout, described as 'soft feel', with curves where the earlier type had offered angular changes of direction. The RS2000 proudly picked up the same type of black-lettering-on-white-faced instruments which had first been seen on the Escort RS Cosworth, while all cars got a new-style steering wheel, an analogue clock in the centre of the fascia, different door bins and other fresh furnishing details.

For the RS2000 there were no major mechanical changes – the 16-valve engine, in particular, was just the same as before – but along with all other Escorts at this juncture there had been a drive to refine the handling, with such details as offset coil springs in the struts, gas-filled dampers,

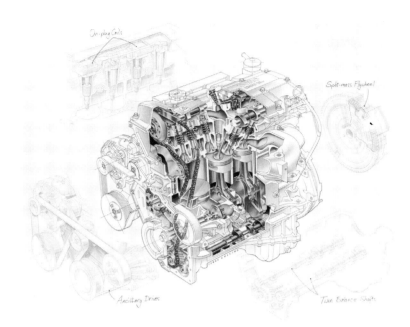

Afterlife. For use in cars like the mid-1990s Scorpio, and late-1990s Galaxy, Ford and Cosworth got together, not only to enlarge the engine to 2.3ltr, but to fit twin 'Lanchester' balancer shafts in the sump. This ultra-smooth variety, however, was never fitted to RS2000s.

stiffened-up front suspension A-arms and an increase in front-suspension wheel castor.

Once again there had been a prices reshuffle. From April 1995, when UK deliveries of the latest RS2000s began, the front-drive car was listed at £14,605, while the RS2000 4×4 cost £15,905 – the price differential this time being £1,300.

Within months, however, the RS2000 came officially under sentence of death. In September 1995 Ford announced that it had finally decided to kill off the RS range. The Escort RS Cosworth would disappear in January 1996, while the RS2000s were to go before the end of that year.

Both, it was stated, would have to be dropped because they could not meet increasingly tough exhaust emission laws and noise regulations, but in truth there was an even more brutal reason than that. Amazing though it might seem, the whole 'RS' concept seemed to have got tired, Ford dealers were

no longer promoting the cars, and sales had dropped to new and depressingly low levels. Ford's Richard Parry-Jones said:

> It's a sad day for hot hatchback fans. For a period at least, there will be no more high-performance Fords.

There was time, but only just time, for die-hard enthusiasts to buy the last of the line, and an *Autocar* group road test of February 1996 showed just how effective the front-wheel-drive RS2000 still was. Not only would it reach an easily-verified 131mph (211km/h), but it was good for hard-driven day-to-day fuel economy of at least 25mpg (11.3l/100km):

> ... the RS2000's six-year-old twin-cam summons more torque and almost as much power from its humbler internals as anything at the money ... only the RS offers a genuinely good driving position. The Ford,

as a result, is the only car in which it is possible to remain truly comfortable for long stints.

Partly this is an upshot of the Ford's fabulous hip-hugging Recaros ... the RS also scores with a typically clear, functional cabin and refreshingly sensible switchgear design. We even approve of the sporty black-on-white instruments ... All three are geared too short for genuine long-distance refinement, Escort especially. But the Ford redeems itself by creating the least wind noise at speed ...

The RS2000 ... is a solid, honest, fast hatchback that neither excels nor disgraces itself in any area dynamically. Yet it has the best cabin, terrific seats and represents fine value.

It was that sort of solid, value-for-money, motoring that Ford's RS badge had always offered, and if it *had* to end, then this was the right way to do it.

When the last RS2000 of all was built before the end of 1996, it brought nearly thirty years of Escort RS history to a close. Although it was not the end of fast Ford motor cars (the 'ST' and 'Racing' types carried on the tradition), it was the end of an era.

Ford spokesmen told us that there would be no more 'RS' badged motor cars in the future, but that didn't mean we had to stop enjoying the cars. As the twenty-first century opened, Ford one-make clubs were thriving, classic RS models were still being rescued, restored and used in great numbers – and there was much enjoyment still to follow.

Ford Escort Performance

This is a summary of the figures achieved by Britain's most authoritative magazine, *Autocar*, of cars supplied for test by Ford over the years:

Model	Escort RS2000 Mk V 1,998cc 150bhp	Escort RS2000 Mk VI 1,998cc 148bhp	Escort RS2000 4×4 Mk VI 1,998cc 148bhp
Max speed (mph)	131	131	128
Accn (sec):			
0–60mph	8.3	8.1	9.4
0–80mph	13.7	13.8	15.6
0–100mph	22.2	22.7	26.0
Standing ¼-mile (sec)	16.4	16.3	17.8
Consumption (mpg)			
Overall	26.4	24.7	28.2
Typical	30	32	32
Kerb weight (lb/kg)	2,477/1,125	2,606/1,182	2,756/1,250
Year tested	1991	1996	1994

Index

AC 3000ME 110
AC Daytona Cobra 96
Advanced Vehicle Operation (AVO)
    12, 157
Alfa Romeo 97, 113, 150
Amblard, Marc 183
Ansdale, Richard 28
Ashcroft, Peter 19, 44, 47, 85–86,
    89, 92, 108–110, 116–117, 141,
    151, 153, 155, 171
Aston Martin 12, 62, 75, 88, 156
Aston Martin DB7 75
Audi Quattro 107–108, 110, 114–115
Auriol, Didier 175
Austin-Rover 42
Autocar (and Motor) 11, 15, 28, 59,
    124, 163, 165, 190, 203
Autosport 109, 142, 145, 148, 156

Bailey, Len 89, 97, 109
Barnett, Bill 19–20, 83–85, 186
Beckett, Terry (later Sir Terence)
    11, 26
Bell, Roger 14
Bennett, Mike 42
Bentley 34
Birmingham (NEC) Motor Show
    125
Birrell, Gerry 53–54, 79, 101, 102
BMC 36, 143
BMW 87, 88, 97, 105–106, 144,
    150, 190
Boxall, Dick 42
Bradley, Terry 132, 152
Braungart, Martin 121
British Leyland 42, 143
British Rally Championship 155,
    174, 176–177, 185
British Saloon (Touring) Car
    Championship 14, 85–86, 88,
    90, 95, 96–97, 136, 141–146,
    149–150, 154, 174

Broad, Ralph 23, 96–97
Broadspeed 84, 86, 90, 96–101,
    103, 104
Brooklyn Ford 142
Buckmaster, Col. Maurice 9

Calton, Harry 9, 15
Carlsson, Erik 36
Chapman, Colin 9–13, 16, 28
Chevrolet Camaro 101
Chitty Chitty Bang Bang 96
Chloride plc 42
Chrysler-UK 32
Clark, Jim 14
Clarke & Simpson 84
Collins, Terry 111, 168, 198
Cossack sponsorship 91, 93
Costin, Mike 165
Cosworth (and Cosworth Racing)
    11, 28, 34–38, 90, 108, 121,
    163–165, 192–193, 201–203
Coventry-Climax 11, 28, 34
Crossland, Len (later Sir Leonard)
    42

Daily Mail 9
Dale-Jones, Graham 147, 152
Datapost 141–144, 148, 149, 150,
    153
DeTomaso Pantera 41
Dobinson, Colin 89, 171, 173–174
Downton Engineering 142–143, 148
Duckworth, Keith 11, 28, 34–37,
    165
Dunabin, Philip 171, 179
Dyble, Rod 53

Eaton Group 42
Endean, Mike 112
Engines:
    105E 165
    Cosworth 1.5ltr Turbo F1 108

Cosworth DFX CART/Indycar 165
Cosworth-Ford BDA 9, 25, 26–28,
    34–35, 37, 43, 77, 86, 101, 102,
    109, 110–111, 165
Cosworth-Ford BDT 111–112
Cosworth-Ford BDT-E 35
Cosworth-Ford DFV F1 12, 165
Cosworth-Ford FVA 19, 25, 28,
    34–35, 97, 165
Cosworth-Ford SCA F2 engine
    165
Cosworth-Ford Scorpio 24-valve
    62, 165, 168
Cosworth-Ford YB family 156,
    161–162, 165, 167, 170–172
Cosworth HB V8 F1 108
CVH 121–124, 133, 137, 139,
    142, 145, 148, 188, 197
Essex V6 43, 111
'Kent' 105E/109E 27, 28, 35,
    45–47, 50, 53, 121
I4 (and RS2000 16-valve)
    189–204
Lotus twin-cam 9–11, 13, 15
Mondeo V6 179
'Pinto' 50, 53, 56, 65, 68, 70, 75,
    79, 81, 82, 118, 189, 192
Zetec 179, 197
Escort Turbo Championship 125,
    127–136, 147, 152
European Rally Championship 170,
    173–176, 185
European Rallycross Championship
    87
European Touring Car
    Championship 87, 89, 96–97,
    102, 104–106, 121, 150

'F2' (Kit Car) Rally Championship
    176–177, 185–186
Fabergé Fiesta Ladies'
    Championship 144

Fabris, 'Edgy' 10, 19
Farren, Malcolm 135
Ferrari 34
FIA/FISA 162, 170, 172, 176, 178
Fiat 131 Abarth 92
Ford factories (and offices):
  AVO (Aveley/South Ockendon)
    21, 23, 26, 29, 31–33, 36–38,
    42–44, 45–60, 61–62, 65, 68,
    75, 80, 86, 119–120
  Boreham 12, 18–20, 21–29, 35,
    42, 61, 75, 81, 89, 91, 94, 96,
    101, 102, 106, 107–118, 121,
    124, 132, 141, 145, 146, 147,
    149, 151–154, 155–156, 168,
    171, 172, 174, 175, 183, 186,
    190
  Bridgend 121
  Cologne 89, 121, 133, 190, 193
  Dagenham 9, 13, 16, 18, 19, 26, 82
  Detroit 108
  Dunton 33, 41, 133, 171, 190
  Halewood 26–31, 38, 41, 42, 44,
    49, 58, 62, 67, 202
  Karmann 75
  Lincoln Cars (Brentford) 10, 20
  Merkenich 181
  Saarlouis 41, 57, 62, 64, 65, 68,
    75, 82, 113, 117, 134
  Warley (Brentwood) 24, 161
Ford models:
  Anglia 105E 11, 16, 22
  Boss Mustang 88
  C100 121
  Capri (and GT) 18, 35, 42, 43, 45,
    47, 54, 68, 78, 104
  Capri 2.8i 62, 68
  Capri RS2600 41, 42, 43, 87, 89,
    102, 103, 108, 121
  Capri RS3100 105, 190
  Classic 109E 11
  Corsair 2000E 16, 47
  Cortina (and GT) 11, 13–20, 22,
    35, 41–43, 45, 47, 54, 68, 78, 96
  Cortina 1600E 21
  Escort 1300E 41
  Escort 1300GT 96–97, 104
  Escort 1300/1600 Sport 65–68,
    73
  Escort Cabriolet 62
  Escort family 23, 26–27, 35, 37,
    49, 50, 78
  Escort Mexico 21, 32, 36, 38,
    42–43, 45–60, 67–68, 85, 87

'Escort RS' 92–95, 97, 103–106,
  107, 110, 115
Escort 'RS1300' 101
Escort RS1600 (J26) 18, 21–44,
  45–60, 67, 68, 85–90, 92, 101,
  104–105, 165, 190
Escort RS1600i 89, 108, 111, 118,
  119–140, 141–145, 148, 150–152
Escort RS1700T (and 'Columbia')
  36, 62, 75, 89, 94, 107–118,
  119, 121, 150–151, 155–156
Escort RS1800 41, 44, 61–82,
  90–95, 102, 105–106, 107, 142,
  165
Escort RS2000 42, 44, 45–60, 68,
  87, 90–91
Escort RS2000 Mk II 44, 61–82,
  90, 96, 119, 121, 131, 189, 191
Escort RS2000 Mk V and Mk VI
  62, 168, 169, 176–177,
  185–186, 187–204
Escort RS2000 Mk V and Mk VI
  4×4 196–204
Escort RS Cosworth (ACE) 12,
  18, 26, 32, 36, 62, 75, 89, 109,
  118, 132, 155–168, 169–184,
  188–189, 198, 199–203
Escort RS Mexico Mk II 44,
  61–82
Escort RS Turbo 36, 62, 75, 111,
  118, 119–140, 142–154, 155,
  161, 188, 193, 195
Escort S 188
Escort 'Turbo Championship' 118
Escort Twin-Cam (J25) 10, 12,
  14, 18, 21–44, 45–46, 49, 60,
  83–86, 88, 89, 96, 97–102
Escort 'World Cup' special 85, 87,
  89
Escort WRC 18, 118, 168, 169,
  178–186
'Escort XR Plus' 190
Escort XR3/XR3i 62, 114, 116,
  117, 119–125, 131–132, 136,
  152, 188, 197, 199–200
Falcon 88, 96
'Fiescort' 107, 110
Fiesta 50, 57, 109, 110, 112, 158,
  192
Fiesta XR2 62, 141–143
Fiesta RS1800 198
Fiesta RS Turbo 139
Focus World Rally Car 179, 184,
  185

Galaxy 201–203
Granada 41–43
GT40 96
GT70 41, 42, 60
Lotus-Cortina (and Cortina Twin
  Cam) 9–11, 13–20, 21–28, 88,
  96
Merkur XR4Ti 143–145, 163
Mondeo 158, 165, 179, 181, 193,
  197, 199–200
Mustang 20, 96
Orion 117, 127, 135, 149
Puma (and Racing) 18, 50, 53, 57
RS200 18, 26, 36, 75, 89, 114,
  116, 117–118, 134, 136, 152,
  154, 155–157
Scorpio 158, 165, 168, 192,
  201–203
Sierra Cosworth 4×4 89,
  155–162, 168, 169–173
Sierra RS (and RS500) Cosworth
  12, 18, 36, 75, 89, 134, 136,
  143, 149, 152, 155–158, 163,
  165–166, 190, 195, 201
Sierra XR4×4 62, 160, 192
Sierra XR4i (and versions) 68,
  118
Taunus 43, 108, 121
Transit van 158, 192
Zephyr 11
Zodiac Mk III 19, 24, 43
Ford Product Strategy Group 116
Ford race and rally drivers:
  Pentti Airikkala 91, 94, 114
  Louise Aitken (later Aitken-
    Walker) 94, 144, 151–152
  Markku Alen 114
  Ove Andersson 20, 23, 28, 83
  Mia Bardolet 161, 169, 170
  Richard Belcher 143
  Patrick Bernardini 175
  Miki Biasion 170–175
  Mohammed Bin Sulayem 176
  Stig Blomqvist 110
  Claude Bourgoignie 102
  Dave Brodie 101
  Russell Brookes 92
  Tony Chappell 84
  Roger Clark 20, 23, 58, 84–88,
    91, 93–94, 96
  Chris Craft 96, 101
  Franco Cunico 173
  Alan Curnow 142–144, 150
  John Davenport 83

Howard Davies 185, 186
Peter Davis 146
François Delecour 169–179, 182
Jorg Denzel 106
Vic Elford 16, 20
Gwyndaf Evans 176–177, 181, 185, 186, 191
Klaus Finotto 105
John Fitzpatrick 90, 96, 97, 101, 102
Gill Fortescue-Thomas 101
Frank Gardner 85–86, 88, 96, 97, 101
Dieter Glemser 104
Daniel Grataloup 173, 178
Armin Hahne 106
Kyosti Hamalainen 142
Paul Hawkins 88
Hans Heyer 103, 105, 106
Chris Hodgetts 142–143
Juha Kankkunen 182–185
Barry Lee 186
Henry Liddon 95
Sebastian Lindholm 186
Richard Longman 122, 136, 141–153
Mark Lovell 136, 145–146, 152–154
Timo Makinen 88, 91–92, 95
Tommi Makinen 174
Nigel Mansell 165
Gerry Marshall 91
Tony Mason 186
Jochen Mass 102
Dave Matthews 97, 101, 102
Jimmy McRae 155
Brian Melia 20
Hannu Mikkola 45, 85, 87, 90–92, 103, 114
Pat Moss 20
Siggi Muller 106
Klaus Niedzweidz 106
Bernard Occelli 175
Gunnar Palm 14, 90
Tony Pond 58
Andy Rouse 101, 102, 143–145
Carlos Sainz 175–176, 182–185
Werner Schommers 106
Michael Schumacher 165
Armin Schwarz 183
Jack Sears 16
David Seigle-Morris 20
Phil Short 152
Simmonite sisters 177

Tiziano Siviero 173
Patrick Snyers 185
Bengt Soderstrom 14, 20, 23
Gilbert Staepelaere 91
Rob Stoneman 147, 152
John Taylor 87, 91–92, 135, 169, 171, 175, 183, 186
Bruno Thiry 174–175, 179, 185
Ari Vatanen 83, 91, 93–94, 96, 106, 112, 114
Bjorn Waldegard 76, 91–92, 97, 102–105, 107
Tom Walkinshaw 75, 79, 82, 101, 103
Sir John Whitmore 96
Malcolm Wilson 94, 114, 117, 151, 152, 170, 171, 174, 183–184
Vince Woodman 97, 101
Ford RS Owners' Club 191
Formula Ford 47
Frankfurt Motor Show 125
Frua 59

Garnier, Peter 15
Geneva Motor Show 75, 199
German Touring Car Championship 103–104
Ghia 110
Gill, Barry 27
Gillitzer, Peter 174, 182
Goater, Pam 186
Gordon Spooner (and GS Engineering) 169, 176, 186
Griffiths, John 82, 90, 105, 111, 117, 132, 152, 155, 186

Hall, Mike 35, 165
Hanson, Peter 101
Harper Engineering 38, 44
Harrison, 'Cuth' 11
Hart, Brian (and engines) 40, 44, 68, 89, 102, 112, 114
Hayes, Walter 9–20, 21–26, 28, 35–42, 115, 119, 121
Haynes, David 11
Haynes of Maidstone 87
Hennessy, Sir Patrick 9
Henson, Syd 19
Hewland, Mike 112
Hill, Graham 29, 43
Hillman Avenger GT and -BRM 32–33
Hillman Imp 118

Holbay Engineering 43
Holman, John (and Holman & Moody) 95
Horrocks, Ray 29, 42, 43
Howe, Bob 24–26, 35, 38, 41–43, 62, 75, 84, 156
Hoyle, Terry 68, 186

JA Prestwich (JAP) 28
Jaguar 11, 13, 20, 34, 106, 165
Jaguar XJ220 75
Janspeed 143, 148
Jones, Mick 19, 21, 89, 109, 117, 186

Karmann 163–164
Kranefuss, Mike 107–108, 110, 121

'Lanchester' balance shafts 203
Lancia (and models) 90–91, 109, 156–158, 165, 172
Lotus 9, 11, 13–15, 28, 62
Lotus Cheshunt factory 13, 16
Lotus models:
  Elan 11, 13, 28
  Elan Plus 2 28
Ludvigsen, Karl 107, 109–110, 113, 115, 119–121, 132, 151
Lutz, Bob 119, 120

Mann, Alan (and Alan Mann Racing) 20, 23, 27, 86, 95–101
Mansfield, Rod 42, 43, 62, 113, 132, 135, 142
Masters, Norman 85
McCrudden, Stuart 33
MCD see RED
Meade, Bill 19–20, 21–22, 25, 83–84, 89, 125, 132, 133, 152, 154, 155, 186
Mercedes-Benz 35, 190
MGA Developments 161
Middle East Rally Championship 176
Mike Taylor Developments 169
Minardi F1 team 165
Mini (family, and Mini-Cooper) 36, 83, 143
Minshaw, Alan 142
Mitsubishi (Ralliart) 174, 183
Moreton, Mike 52, 59, 61–62, 75, 80, 155–160
Morgan 45

Motor 14, 18
Motor Racing Research 88
Motoring News 36, 79
Mountune 166, 172
M-Sport 183–186
Mundy, Harry 11, 15, 28

National Motor Museum 93
Neerpasch, Jochen 121

Opel (and models) 94, 115
Oros, Joe 57

Parry-Jones, Richard 168, 202–203
Penske, Roger 108
Penske-Kranefuss Racing 108
Peter Sellers Racing team 89
Peugeot 143
Philadelphia's City Hall 191
Pinske, Lothar 121, 132
Platt, Alan 20, 23
Porsche (and models) 85, 109, 110,
    113, 156

RAC MSA 94
Radiopaging 145, 152
Rallies:
    1,000 Lakes 85, 87, 93, 94, 95,
        142, 174
    Acropolis 87, 91, 92, 93, 94, 95,
        102, 164, 173, 175, 176, 182,
        184
    Argentina 173, 174, 176
    Australia 173, 176
    Austrian Alpine 95
    Brazil 93, 94, 95
    Circuit of Ireland 84–85, 94, 151,
        153
    Cumbria (Pirelli) 177
    Cyprus 93, 95
    Czechoslovakian 152
    Gulf London 20
    Hadrian Centurion 170
    Indonesia 176, 184
    Jim Clark 86
    Manx (Isle of Man) 154, 177
    Mintex 93, 151, 152
    Monte Carlo 14, 92, 94, 96, 104,
        157, 169, 172, 173, 174, 175,
        177, 178, 179, 184
    Morocco 91
    New Zealand (Heatway) 87, 91,
        92, 93, 95, 173, 184
    Portugal 91, 92, 95, 173, 174

PTV 179
Quebec 91, 92, 93, 95
RAC (Lombard-RAC) 20, 36, 86,
    87, 91, 92, 95, 103, 151, 152,
    154, 157, 174, 176, 177, 185, 186
Safari 85, 86, 87, 90, 91, 92, 95,
    97, 121, 157
San Remo 28, 83, 173, 174, 176,
    186
Scottish 87, 93, 153
Southern Cross 91
Spain (Catalunya) 173, 175, 176
Spa-Sofia-Liège 20
Swedish 20, 94, 144, 175, 182, 184
Talavera 161, 169
Total (South Africa) 91, 95
Tour de Corse (Corsica) 155, 157,
    173, 175, 184
Tour de France 20, 96
Tour of Britain 58, 87, 95, 96
Tulip 95
Ulster 153, 181
Welsh 20, 93, 151
West Cork 153
World Cup (*Daily Mirror*) 43, 45,
    46, 85, 86, 88–89, 95
Rallye Sport (RS) and dealers 9, 42
RAS Sport (and RAS-Ford) 174
RED (Rally Engineering
    Development) 144, 151, 153,
    154
Reynard 181
Reynolds, Charles 92
Richard Longman Engineering
    142–143
Rocky 191
Rolls-Royce 35
Rootes Group 75
Rothmans sponsorship 83, 93–94,
    106
Rover 144
Rule, Johnnie 19
Russell, Jim 88

Sauber F1 team 165
Scheele, Nick 38
SEAT 177
Smith, Mike 154
Spanish Gravel Rally
    Championship 170
Special Vehicle Engineering (Ford)
    42, 62–63, 75, 113–115, 118,
    132, 135, 137, 142, 152,
    157–164, 167, 190, 191, 201

Stewart F1 team 165
Stroud, Nigel 181
Subaru (and models) 177
Sunday Dispatch 11
Sutton, David (and David Sutton
    [Cars]) 84, 91, 92, 93–94, 103,
    106
Sytner, Frank 150

Taylor, Henry 20, 21–28, 36, 42, 62,
    84
TC Prototypes 160
Team Lotus 14
Telnack, Jack 61, 78
Thompson, John 160
Toyota 150, 172, 173
Trakstar 154
Trotman, Alex (later Sir Alex) 42
Turner, Stuart 12, 35–36, 42, 52,
    59, 61–62, 75, 85, 89, 95, 108,
    115–117, 121, 132, 134, 151,
    155–156, 169–170, 186
TVR 45
Twice Lucky 36
TWR 75

Vauxhall 75
Vegantune 97
Vivian, David 190
Vokins, Robin 183
Volvo 148
VW (and models) 142, 150, 195

Walton, Jeremy 64
Weslake 35
Wheeler, John 75, 109–118,
    155–162, 171, 173
Whitaker, Martin 182
Wilkinson, Allan 89, 91, 109
Willment, John 88
Wood, David 103
World Rally Cars 178–186
World Rally Championship (Makes
    and Manufacturers) 90–93,
    105–109, 170, 172–176,
    183–186
World Sports Car Championship
    96

Zakowski, Erich 104
Zakspeed 62, 86–87, 94, 103–106,
    121